A History of
NORTHAMPTONSHIRE

The interior of Braybrooke church in the 1930s. The vamping horn and wooden effigy are now in the Harborough Museum.

THE DARWEN COUNTY
HISTORY SERIES

A History of
NORTHAMPTONSHIRE
AND THE SOKE OF PETERBOROUGH

R.L. Greenall

Phillimore

2000

Published by
PHILLIMORE & CO. LTD.
Shopwyke Manor Barn, Chichester, West Sussex

First published 1979
Second edition 2000

ISBN 1 86077 147 5

Printed and bound in Great Britain by
BUTLER AND TANNER LTD.
Frome, Somerset

Contents

List of Illustrations

Frontispiece: The interior of Braybrooke church in the 1930s.

List of Colour Illustrations

Illustration Acknowledgements

I express my appreciation to the following repositories and individuals for permission to reproduce illustrations in their collections, or provided by them: The British Museum, 9, 14, 15; Bruce Bailey, 1, 2, 4, 6, 8, 10, 11, 16, 17, 20, 26, 28, 31, 32, 34, 41, 42, 46, 65, 75, 77, 80, 82-4, 90, 91, 99, 103, 111, 115, 118, 126, 127, 130, 131, 137, 139, 145-7, 150, 151, 161, 164, 167, 170, 173-5; Alan Burman, 71; Cambridge University Centre for Aerial Photography, 24 and 35; By kind permission of His Grace the Duke of Buccleuch and Queensberry, K.T., 76; English Heritage, 21 and 39; Glenn Foard, 19; David Hall, 23, 128 and 129; The Museum of Rural Life, Reading University, 134; Northampton Labour Party, 168; Northampton Museum & Art Gallery, 93, 158; Northamptonshire Libraries and Information Service, 30, 38, 58, 60-2, 66, 68-70, 72, 73, 85, 86, 92, 98, 100-2, 105, 107, 108, 112, 114, 117, 119-21, 123-5, 133, 135, 136, 138, 141-3, 149, 151-3, 156, 165, 171, 172, 179; Northamptonshire Archaeology, 18; Northamptonshire Record Office, frontispiece, II, VII, 8, IX, XIII, XIV, 29, 40, 44, 95, 106, 125 and 177; the late Fred Moore, 157; David Parsons, 22; John Williams, I; illustrations 43, 44, 57 and 59 are from *Architectural Notices of the Churches of the Archdeaconry of Northampton* (1849); 12 and 13 are from Edmund Artis, *The Durobrivae of Antoninus* (1828); 49 and 52 are from George Baker, *The History and Antiquities of Northamptonshire*, I (1823-30); and 27, 67 and 74 are from W.H. Hyett, *Sepulchral Monuments ... Within the County of Northampton* (1817). The rest are from the author's collection.

Acknowledgements

In revising this book and selecting a range of new illustrations for it I am indebted to many people and organisations, but especially to the County Record Office and Northamptonshire Libraries and Information Service. The richness of their collections and the courtesy and willingness of their staff to go out of their way to help make working in Northamptonshire an abiding pleasure. In particular, I would like to thank Rachel Watson and Sue Groves at the Record Office and Terry Bracher and Colin Eaton at Abington Street Library. A special thankyou is due to Bruce Bailey who drew several new maps and whose maps and drawings are a major contribution to the 2nd edition of this book.

I should also thank the many people attending adult education courses over the years who have provided information and insight into Northamptonshire's local history and generously allowed me to make copies of material they have preserved and collected.

Preface

It is now upwards of twenty years since the first edition of this book appeared. In this time Northamptonshire has changed and so has our knowledge of its history. What the planners envisioned in the 1960s and '70s has largely came to pass. However, the era of 'New Town' expansion was completed in the '80s, and the Development Corporations which masterminded it are long gone. Yet development, sanctioned by local government and carried out by the private sector, continues. In the New Town era Northamptonshire's road system was improved and more new roads have been built since. Many a town and village has received its by-pass, creating out-of-town industry and retailing. On the other hand, Corby no longer has a steelworks and the once ubiquitous production of footware has continued to contract. With their passing and decline, Northamptonshire life has lost some of its traditional defining characteristics. Inexorably, it has been drawn more completely into the affluent embrace of the South East. Yet much of its old character survives. If some small towns and villages have grown markedly, selected places of special architectural or historical interest have had their development restricted. Some of the landed estates remain in the same family ownership as in 1979 (or indeed 1879). And the spires of the 'county of spires and squires' are well-maintained, despite the difficulties faced by those in whose care they lie.

In the past twenty years archaeologists and historians have greatly added to our knowledge. The researches of such people as John Williams, Glenn Foard, Tony Brown, Christopher Taylor, Michael Franklin and David Hall are casting fascinating new light on the early history of the county. The Inspectors and other workers in the Royal Commission on Historical Monuments have just about completed their superb survey of the archaeological sites and monuments, churches and country houses of Northamptonshire. The Victoria County History, dormant since the 1930s, has been revived and new volumes are in preparation. Most recently, a magisterial survey of the medieval stained glass in the churches of the county has appeared. Not all periods have been so well-served: few historians seem to be researching Tudor, Stuart and Georgian Northamptonshire, though this may well change. Historical research, like everything else in modern life, is at the mercy of contingency.

The present writer has been a Northamptonshire-watcher since 1965. When I arrived I knew little of the place, but was soon aware of the strong sense of their own history felt by Northamptonshire people.

Thereafter, I became much involved in local history through teaching and involvement with the County Record Society. Our times have also seen much activity on the amateur front, especially the rise in the study of family history, and the Millennium has generated a number of publications by local history societies. One hopes that all those interested in local history will welcome this new edition of *A History of Northamptonshire*.

RON GREENALL

Note

In planning this book one problem was whether or not to include the Soke of Peterborough, which severed its connections with Northampton in 1888, and since 1974 has been part of the enlarged county of Cambridgeshire. Because this connection was so ancient, and so important to early history of the county, there really was no question that Peterborough could be excluded: a history without the abbey, cathedral and Soke would have been manifestly incomplete and inadequate.

1

Northamptonshire Before the Norman Conquest

Land and Landscape

To anyone looking at Northamptonshire on the map, an inescapable feature is its singular shape. It is a roughly eliptical tract of territory about seventy miles long and a mere twenty miles or so at its broadest. In matters of travel it seems to have been designed for maximum inconvenience, for though it is only seventy to eighty miles from London, it lies athwart, rather than along, national lines of communication. This configuration of the county is determined partly by history, but also by the geography and by the geology of the area. Physically its backbone is a belt of Liassic rocks and Oolitic limestone, part of the great Jurassic ridge which runs right across England from Dorset to the Humber. From the limestone, particularly the Lincolnshire limestone found north of Kettering, is quarried some of the finest and most enduring building stone in England. This was used not only for Northamptonshire's own parish churches and villages, but further afield for such buildings as the

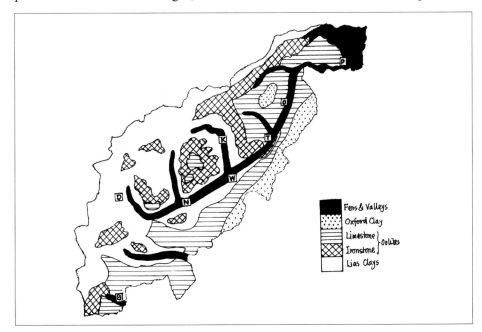

1 *Geological map of Northamptonshire.*

2 *Source of the River Avon at Naseby.*

great medieval monasteries of eastern England and the colleges of Cambridge. The rest of the solid geology of the area is basically Oxford clay, though we find widespread overlaying of Glacial boulder clay, and gravels and alluvium in the river valleys.

Considerable stretches of the county boundaries are formed by rivers. Whilst Northamptonshire is part of the great Midland plain, with only two or three hills as high as 700 ft. above sea level, its geography is much influenced by the gentle uplands to the west and north of Northampton. The scarp and dipslope of the Northampton Heights form the watershed for river systems which have more than merely local significance. The Avon rises some six hundred feet above sea level in Naseby and flows north and then west, forming the county boundary with Leicestershire, as it begins its long journey to the Bristol Channel. The Welland rises in the next parish, flows north down the scarp face and then eastwards, forming another 30-mile stretch of the boundary of the county and the old Soke of Peterborough on its way to the Wash. In the other direction down the dipslope flow the Cherwell, the Great Ouse, and the Tove, each in turn acting as the county boundary. Locally, the most important of all the streams of the dipslope are the Nene and its tributaries. The Nene is the county's principal waterway, the county town is at the confluence of its two feeders, and most of the other towns of importance are at a crossing or a confluence of it. The Nene Valley is the heart of the county, and contains the richest arable land, its most ancient settlements and finest medieval churches.

3 *Working Collyweston slate with a 'claiving' hammer. Collyweston slate is a fairly easily splittable limestone formerly used extensively for roofing stone houses between Great Weldon and Stamford.*

The Nene Valley and the Northampton Heights form two well-defined geographical regions of the county, the latter (from the end of the Middle Ages) as noted for grazing as the Nene Valley was for corn growing. Another, really an extension of the uplands, is the area in the south-west corner of the county, known to the geographers as the Wolds. Here the hills, though no higher than those to the north of Daventry, are steeper and the land more undulating. This area, too, became famous for its pastures. Two further regions are areas of former forest and woodland. To the south of Northampton and the Nene is a landscape, once heavily wooded, in which there are still three tracts of forest—Whittlewood, Salcey, and Yardley Chase. Another woodland area, Rockingham Forest, is in the

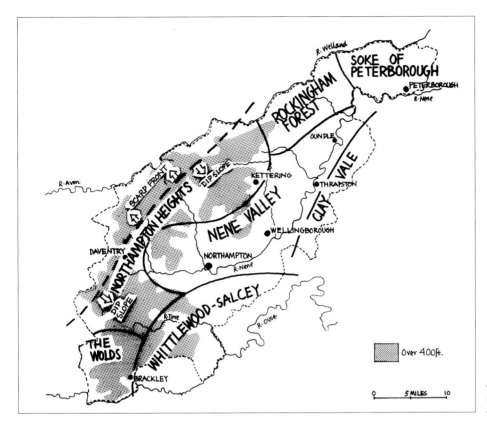

4 *The geographical regions of Northamptonshire.*

north of the county: in early times this region, then bounded by the Welland on the north, the Nene to the south, Rockingham and Kettering on the west, and Stamford and Wansford on the east, was, like Whittlewood, a favourite hunting ground of the medieval kings. Since the Middle Ages it has been massively disafforested, but to this day vestigial or replanted tracts of woodland remain. A sixth natural region is the area between the central Nene Valley and the border with Bedfordshire and Cambridgeshire. It is entirely on Oxford clay and in ancient times was the forest of *Bruneswald*, a fastness in which the outlaw Hereward the Wake hid himself from the Normans. Today, this rather flat arable landscape is little wooded, though its ancient name survives in that of the village of Newton Bromswold.

The final geographical division of the ancient (though not the modern) county is that of the Soke of Peterborough. Dominated by the cathedral city, its geography is summed up in the name of the ancient hundred, *Nassaburgh*. When the tenth-century monks re-founded their monastery—which was at first called simply Burgh—they chose a site at the end of a limestone promontory, 'the ness of Burgh', projecting into the fen, and the town which grew up outside its gates prospered as a market where the products of the fen, the forest and the field were bought and sold.

5 *The Peterborough district, from the map accompanying Morton's* Natural History of Northamptonshire, *1712. It shows Mortons Leame and the Nene beyond Peterborough before it was navigated. Whittlesey Mere was not drained until the 1850s.*

The essential point, is, however, that whichever geographical region of Northamptonshire we consider, the soil is rich and productive. Where it is less good for cereals it is good for grazing; virtually nowhere is it barren or intractable. As Thomas Fuller, one of its native sons, wrote in his *Worthies of England* in the 17th century, the land 'is as fruitful and populous as any in England … there is as little waste ground in this, as in any county in England (no mosses, mears, fells, heaths … where elsewhere fill so many shires with much emptiness); Northamptonshire being an apple, without a core to be cut out, or rind to be pared away'.[1]

Prehistoric and Roman Northamptonshire

In prehistoric times much of the landscape of Northamptonshire was intractable woodland, and it is the gravel terraces of the Nene Valley and the trackways of the Jurassic ridge which yield most evidence of early man. The 'Jurassic way' in particular is seen a route of major importance declining only with the creation of the Roman road system.

Evidence of the existence of very early man in the county is not plentiful, though the small pear-shaped flint axe-heads and bone tools of the Palaeolithic period have been found in at least fourteen places in the Nene Valley, and there have been finds of mammoth bones and musk-ox bones in the gravels. Similarly there have only been a few finds of the small flint blades used by the intermediate hunter-fisher groups of the

Mesolithic period. The intractable nature of the country is shown by the relatively scanty evidence of the flint axes and other tools of the first farming and herding communities who appear in the early Neolithic period, about the third millennium B.C. The first major evidence of settlement of Neolithic farmers in the county is at Fengate, Peterborough, described as 'the richest multiperiod site in eastern England'. At Fengate, not only is there evidence of an early Neolithic site, but also of a larger later Neolithic settlement which produced a distinctive coarse decorated pottery known as 'Peterborough' ware, with a more developed form known as 'Fengate' or 'grooved ware'. It is assumed that the people who used this pottery were connected with those who erected the vast ceremonial monuments in south-west England, a contact presumably made along the trade routes of the Jurassic way. It is believed that the ditched site with double causeways at Thornhaugh, near Wansford, revealed in air photographs, is possibly a forerunner of the later 'henge' monuments found at such sites as Avebury. Also associated with the 'Peterborough culture', and further evidence of prehistoric trade over long distances, are the great polished ceremonial stone axe-heads from 'factories' at Great Langdale in Cumbria and from Dartmoor, which have been found in at least eight places in the county.

6 Bronze-Age dagger from Perio, Southwick

The late Neolithic Fengate site, too, has yielded up fragments of the pottery of the earliest Bronze-Age people, the so-called 'Beaker folk', from about 2100-1800 B.C., though their pottery has not been found further up the valley of the Nene. About 1800 to 1700 B.C. there followed another wave of Bronze-Age people who did penetrate the Nene

7 The Iron-Age hill-fort of Hunsbury, about 1970. As part of the Southern district of the Northampton Development area, the hill is now surrounded by new housing and busy roads.

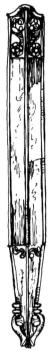

Valley, and whose pottery has been found as far up as Brixworth. It was these folk who constructed barrows for their dead along the Jurassic ridge. About the year 1000 B.C. there came the introduction of settled farmsteads linked to field systems by a race of warrior-farmers who used skilfully-wrought bronze weapons. In Northampton Museum there is a fine collection of their socketed axes, slashing swords, spear-heads and urns.

About the year 500 B.C. the Iron Age was introduced by people from the Continent in the form of the 'Hallstatt' culture. Here Fengate comes into the picture again: recent excavation has revealed a large farming settlement spread over a wide area and overlaying the earlier Bronze-Age community. In the next century settlers began to spread westwards into the upland zone, and it was in this period that a series of hill-forts were constructed at Arbury Camp, Rainsborough Camp, Borough Hill, Castle Dykes, Guilsborough, Irthlingborough and, most notable of all, Hunsbury Hill, across the river, south of modern Northampton. Recently archaeologists have added two more possible hill-forts to this list: Arbury Hill (Badby) and Thenford. Colonised by several generations of iron-smelters, Hunsbury has yielded finds which show its people traded over considerable distances. Fine burnished bowls with incised designs introduced by later Iron-Age people of the La Tène culture, two fine brooches from Yorkshire, decorated with curvilinear La

8 *Celtic scabbard from Hunsbury Hill.*

Tène designs, iron currency bars of the Dobunni people of the Forest of Dean and magnificent sword scabbards of the first century B.C. have been excavated here. From Rainsborough Camp came a fine harness-fitting, decorated with an enamelled 'lyre' pattern of the same period. And at Desborough, a most magnificent Celtic bronze mirror from the workshop of the Dobunni, roughly contemporary with the Roman conquest, was found.

It seems that, by the time of the last wave of Celtic migrants from Europe, the hill sites had fallen into disuse, for little evidence of these newcomers has been found in them. Early in the first century B.C. most of Northamptonshire became part of the territory of the Belgic Catuvellauni. Their chieftain, Cunobelin, established his centre first near St Albans, and then, with his capture of Colchester, became a major force in South Britain.

9 *The Desborough Mirror. One of the great treasures of Romano-British archaeology, now in the British Museum.*

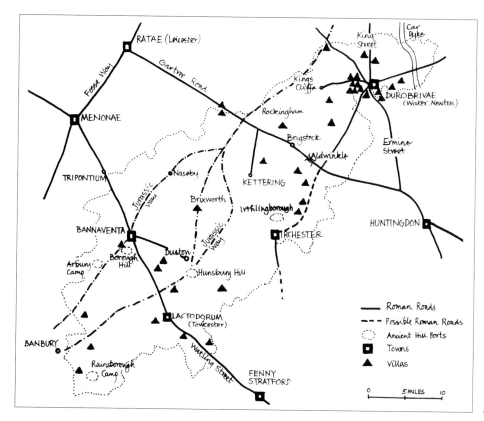

10 *Prehistoric and Roman Northamptonshire.*

Northamptonshire seems to have been his most northerly possession, for Leicestershire was in the territory of the non-Belgic Corieltauvi, and East Anglia belonged to the Iceni. The chief evidence of Belgic settlement in the county comes from Duston, where finds include some gold coins of the Catuvellauni. Northamptonshire did not long remain part of that Celtic kingdom, for the Catuvellauni were overthrown when Colchester was captured by the Romans after the invasion of A.D. 43. The Roman armies then divided into three expeditionary forces, and Ermine Street, skirting the fens, marks the line of advance northwards of the Ninth Legion. To guard the point where it crossed the Nene a fort was erected at Water Newton; the Romans called it Durobrivae, 'the fort by the ford'. Later on a bigger military camp was constructed on the north bank of the Nene further down river at Longthorpe.

Under the Romans, the first century A.D. was a time of prosperity and settlement in the lower Nene Valley, in the area between King's Cliffe and Peterborough. Durobrivae became a thriving market town, the centre of an important part of Roman Britain. Peasant farming in the fens, drained by Roman drainage dykes, and a network of villas and their estates in the fertile Nene Valley produced large quantities of cereals. Centred on Castor was a considerable pottery industry, which in the second and third centuries A.D. produced black glazed beakers and finely decorated vessels,

11 *Castor-ware 'Hunt Cup'.*

12 *Mosaic floor from Pail Grounds, Helpstone, from E.A. Artis,* The Durobrivae of Antoninus, *1828.*

often with lively hunting scenes. Following the decline in the production of Samian-ware in Gaul, Castor-ware was exported to the northern part of the Empire on a considerable scale. In this period, too, the Romano-British exploited the iron-ore deposits in the Rockingham forest, the stone quarries at Barnack, Wittering and Collyweston, and fine mosaics were produced by the so-called 'Durobrivan school'. Yet, despite the undoubted importance of the Castor district as an industrial and grain-producing centre, Northamptonshire seems not to have been a recognisable tribal unit under the Romans. A territory without its own civitas capital (there have been scarcely any Roman finds in Northampton), it lay between the Corieltauvi with their civitas capital at Leicester and the Catuvellauni, whose civitas capital was at St Albans. Nor was there a coloniae or legionary fortress in Roman Northamptonshire.

13 *Hunting deer with greyhounds. Motifs from a Roman Castor-ware pot, drawn in the early 19th century for Edmund Artis' book on Durobrivae.*

No other part of Roman Northamptonshire seems to have been as densely peopled as Durobrivae and its district. Modern archaeology, however, continues to reveal evidence of extensive settlement on villa-based estates and in or near Roman 'small towns'. In the west the axis of settlement was the great military road, Watling Street. At Lactodorum (Towcester) a walled town was developed on the site of the earlier Belgic settlement, and at Bannaventa (Whilton) the second of the three Roman towns of Northamptonshire was established. It was linked by road to Duston where the Belgic settlement increased in importance under the Romans, and became a centre of pewtermaking and metal-working. The story of the Romans in Northamptonshire cannot yet be fully told. The Longthorpe fortress was only excavated in 1961 and the Peterborough Expansion Area is still revealing new information. Recently, however, the pattern of settlement in central Northamptonshire has become clearer. Excavations at Brigstock revealed circular votive shrines, and gravel digging at Aldwinkle uncovered the wooden bridge and causeway by which Gartree Road crossed the Nene on its way to link Leicester to Ermine Street. The connections of the third of Northamptonshire's Roman towns, Irchester, will no doubt become clearer in the future.

In the late fourth century the defences of Imperial Rome became overstretched, and in 410 the legions were withdrawn from Britain, leaving the Romano-British to defend their island themselves. Shortly after, Vortigern, the British 'overking', enlisted Germanic barbarians under Hengist to strengthen his defences against the threat of a seaborne invasion by the Picts. Their location had nothing to do with 'routes' of 'invaders' who 'penetrated up valleys'. These first English were stationed where Vortigern wanted them, along the main roads from the Thames Valley to the Humber, to guard inland Britain. Those who settled in Northamptonshire were principally Angles.

14 *Romano-British stone-carved head from Towcester, now in the British Museum.*

15 *Fourth-century Christian silver Chi-Rho leaves, from the Water Newton Treasure discovered in 1979, and now in the British Museum.*

The Pictish invasion never materialised. Civil war, and not foreign invasion, destroyed the Romano-British state and opened Britain to the English. When, in 442, the British leaders quarrelled and failed to pay their mercenaries, Hengist launched a savage revolt from his base in Kent. The military resources of the Anglo-Saxons were limited, but they called in support from Germany, and after 10 years of war emerged supreme in Lincolnshire, East Anglia, Kent and Sussex. Not only did they successfully establish these bridgeheads, but their revolt shattered Romano-British society and ruined its economy. In Northamptonshire the end seems not to have been violent. The ramparts at Towcester fell into the ditch; villas and towns were abandoned; the rich buried their valuables, and there have been a number of finds of such treasure from this period. One of the most notable was made at Water Newton in 1975. Its interest derives chiefly from the fact that not only is it a hoard of fine late third- or early fourth-century silver plate, but many of the items bear Chi-Rho and Alpha-and-Omega monograms, making it the earliest hoard of Christian treasure found anywhere in the world. It seems that it was perhaps buried by a rich Christian who had a shrine in his villa, and hid the silver either during the collapse of 442, or possibly earlier, during the Diocletian persecution.

By the end of the fifth century A.D., all of what later became Northamptonshire as far west as Watling Street was in the hands of the English. In the sixth century the area between later Daventry and Banbury fell to their armies.

Anglo-Saxon and Danish Northamptonshire

The economic and social consequences of the collapse of Romano-British civilisation were disastrous, analogous to the massive population fall and economic recession which was to come in the Later Middle Ages. In the 5th century Britain reverted to the situation it was in in A.D. 43 when the Romans came. With the population fall, the agricultural system collapsed and the monetary economy disintegrated. Villas were abandoned and towns fell into disuse. It was to take another 500 years for the economic system to recover.

'The Dark Ages' were a period of profound discontinuities. Over the recent past some archaeologists and landscape historians have argued that this economic and social collapse has been exaggerated. Archaeology has shown that some people continued to live in Roman towns, but they were not the English. Some excavated villas, such as the one at Brixworth, show activity in the Saxon period, but this seems to reflect Romano British land-owners holding on rather than English occupation. And there are a number of places where later manorial sites are in close proximity to villas, for example at Wollaston, Marston Trussell, Brackley and Higham Ferrers, though this may well be as much due to their favoured locations as to continuity. Where continuity exists it was on the best agricultural land, especially in the river valleys. But even here discontinuity is the norm. In the words of Brown and Foard, 'The pattern of medieval fields bears no relationship to the underlying Iron Age and Roman field systems as revealed as crop marks in aerial photography'.[2]

16 *Anglo-Saxon brooch from Newnham.*

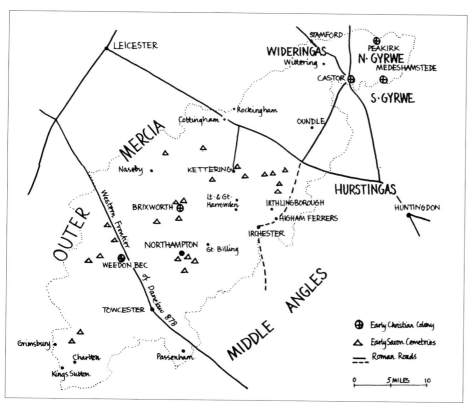

17 *Anglo-Saxon and Danish Northamptonshire.*

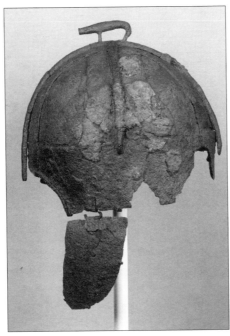

18 The seventh-century warrior's helmet found at Wollaston in 1997.

Many Roman sites fail to yield up any examples of Saxon pottery. In early Anglo-Saxon times there was a fundamental change in the rural settlement pattern and land use.

On the 'permeable geologies' (the best and most easily worked land) the pattern of early Anglo-Saxon settlement revealed by systematic field-walking is that of an intensive but dispersed occupation, in the form of single farmsteads. In contrast, on the more marginal land of the main valley watersheds, there is an almost complete loss of settlement. These claylands were cleared and farmed in the Iron Age, but almost without exception produce no evidence of Early to Middle Anglo-Saxon occupation. It seems that withdrawal from these areas took place at the same time as villas and towns were being deserted. The only exception seems to be in Rockingham Forest where an iron industry continued to exist from the Iron Age to the end of the Middle Ages, evidence of its continuation being provided by pottery found in the slag on ironworking sites.

By the seventh century the people of what was to become Northamptonshire had become part of the Midland kingdom of Mercia, which, under its last pagan king, Penda, took the leadership of the warring English kingdoms in A.D. 633. In the century and a half before that, the Angles had either killed, driven out or absorbed the native British and settled down as farmers who were also called upon to be warriors in Mercia's campaigns. Documentary evidence, notably the 'Tribal Hidage' (whose date is disputed), gives the names of a few of the tribal groups, the *Wideringas,* whose name perhaps survives in Wittering, and the *North and South Gyrwe,* who probably lived around what was later to be Peterborough. How these tribal groups formed into territories and became part of the kingdom of Mercia is not clear, though archaeological finds occasionally throw light on them. One that thrilled archaeologists and captured the imagination of the public was the discovery in 1997 in a gravel quarry at Wollaston of the grave of a high-status Anglo-Saxon warrior. Dating from about A.D. 650, it contained a bowl, a highly patterned steel sword, which had been kept in a wool-lined scabbard and a helmet with nose guard and crescent-shaped cheek protectors. It was only the fourth such warrior's helmet to be found for this period, and what excited much interest was that it had a crest on it in the form of a boar, probably representing the Germanic deity Freyr, similar to one

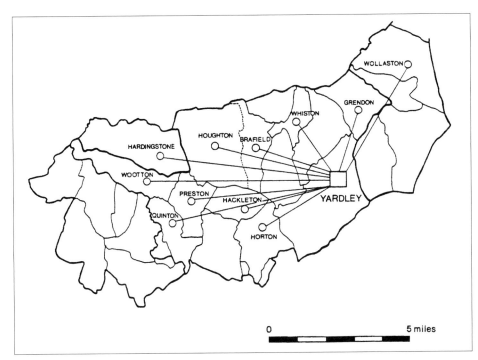

19 *An Anglo-Saxon Soke: Yardley and its dependent townships. Glenn Foard has shown that this great estate later became the hundred of Wymersley (whose boundaries are drawn in heavier line), except for Wollaston, which became part of the hundred of Higham, and Hardingstone, which became part of the hundred of Collingtree.*

referred to in the near-contemporary Anglo-Saxon poem, *Beowulf*. These were the accoutrements of a tribal chief or princeling.

Northamptonshire belongs to that part of Lowland England characterised by nucleated villages once surrounded by great open-fields. This pattern is the legacy of the Anglo Saxons and was certainly in place before the time of the Norman Conquest. How and when did townships—villages, their fields and their boundaries—develop out of the scattered individual farms of the original settlement? The archaeological evidence points to three distinct phases: *nucleation*, *replanning* (which took place in the 9th and 10th centuries) and *infilling* (which went on up to about 1300).

Evidence from a major excavation at Raunds and archaeological work in other places shows that the move from scattered farms to nucleated sites took place in the Middle Saxon period, between *c*.650 and *c*.850. Some of these settlements show evidence of having been planned, whilst others were laid out more irregularly, sometimes around greens or oval spaces (some later utilised as churchyards, as at Greens Norton, Brackley, Gretton and Weldon), though greens villages are not common in Northamptonshire.

In the 5th and 6th centuries A.D. under the kings of Mercia a tribute-based economic system emerged through which, at certain central places, supplies were rendered in kind to royal reeves. These places were often the centres of 'Sokes', extensive estates in which a number of sub-settlements were dependent on a main centre belonging to the king. The work of Glenn Foard and others has identified some 32 such sokes.

20 *Sculpture of Christ in majesty, Barnack church.*

Later, some of these extensive estates became the bases of hundreds, the administrative divisions into which the future county was to be divided. From the Middle Saxon period these sokes were broken down into smaller land units by a process of manorialisation, though some (such as Rothwell, Finedon and Yardley Hastings) survived until the time of Domesday Book, in which their dependencies are recorded. It is by 'back-projecting' from this and other sources that the pattern of Anglo-Saxon land and administrative units has been reconstructed. Some of these soke centres were later to become prominent towns such as Northampton, Brackley, Higham Ferrers, Towcester, Rothwell and Oundle. Others, however, like Brigstock, Brixworth, Fawsley, Gretton, Passenham and Yardley Hastings became ordinary villages, whose ancient importance is known only to antiquarians and historians.

At a higher level than sokes there is evidence that suggests that Mercian Northamptonshire was divided into three 'provinces', centred on the major estate centres of King's Sutton in the south, Northampton in the centre and Oundle in the north. Remarkable evidence of the importance of Northampton was revealed in the excavations carried out by John Williams and the archaeological unit of the Northampton Development Corporation in the 1970s close by the east end of St Peter's church. Here they found evidence of a stone-built seventh-century church below the present St Peter's (itself one of the most ancient churches in the area).

21 *The findings of the Northampton Development Corporation's Archaeological Unit in the 1970s. They discovered the footings of a Middle Saxon minster below, and projecting beyond, the east end of the present church of St Peter. Mysterious circular concrete-like structures, unique in archaeology, thought to be the bases of mortar mixers used for the work on substantial stone buildings, were also found. And the footings of two great halls, or 'palaces', were revealed. These are thought to have belonged to the kings of Mercia, and were the centre of a great estate based on Northampton. The hill on which they stand is almost certainly the site of the first settlement at Northampton. The earlier hall (seventh-century) was of timber; the later one had stone footings.*

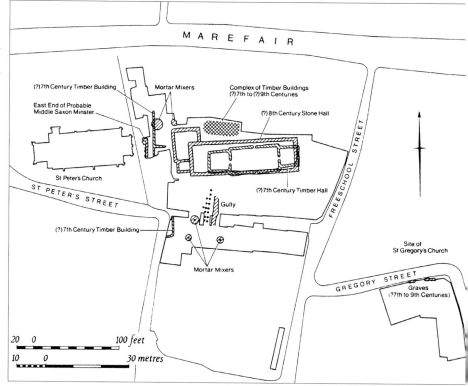

and, in close proximity, the presence of a great Anglo-Saxon 'palace', indicating the presence of a major administrative centre. There is also a well-known reference in the writings of Bede to Oundle being a 'province', and another to an ancient administrative unit called the 'eight hundreds of Oundle'.

The conversion of the Mercians took place when the first christian king, Peada, succeeded his pagan father, Penda, after the latter had been killed in battle with the Northumbrians in A.D. 654. Peada established a monastery at *Medeshamstede* (Peterborough). Before the creation of the parochial system (between the 11th and 13th centuries) the conversion and cure of souls was based on regional 'minsters', each of which administered a large *parochia* or territory and was probably staffed by a college of clergy. Only a few of the 'old minsters' are known for certain. Brixworth is the most famous, largely through the remarkable evidence of its fabric, but it seems certain that others, such as Kings Sutton, Oundle, Rothwell, St Peter's, Northampton, Brigstock, Nassington and Geddington were associated with royal estate centres. That these minsters once served places which later acquired their own churches and parishes is shown by the fact that, for long after the Conquest, dependent churches had to bury their dead in the old minster churchyard, pay dues to and otherwise avoid infringing privileges of the mother church.

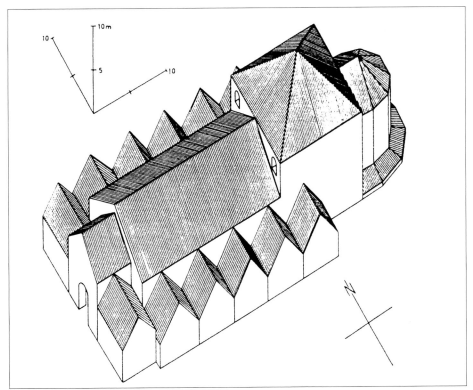

22 *Isometric reconstruction by D. Parsons showing how the old minster of Brixworth might have looked at an unspecified date in the Anglo-Saxon period. At the west end a broad 'narthex' incorporates a central porch of two storeys. The nave is lower than at present and is surrounded by individual* porticus *or chapels. The choir rises above the nave and forms a low tower. At the east end there is an apse, surrounded by the roof of an underground ambulatory. (Compare this with colour plate II, facing p.33.)*

As well as major soke settlements, there were other 'central sites'. Historians recognise one such in the Middle Saxon 'burhs', the defended residences of important men. Others were meeting places of the folk, or the sites of old minsters, and are sometimes found to be linked to soke centres. Rothwell, a royal estate centre with an old minster, was paired with Desborough, a place which has yielded princely burials. Passenham and Higham Ferrers were estate centres in 1086, apparently remnants of earlier royal sokes. Irthlingborough was the centre of a Middle Saxon estate, whilst Finedon was the meeting place of the 'Thing' or folk moot. These central places sometimes had a range of specialist settlement around them. Kings Sutton (the *king's south tun)* has its *priest's tun, ceorl's tun* and *east cote*, while others have their *wics, steads, cotes* and *thorpes.*

The basic element in rural organisation was the *township,* the land unit which enabled a community to be self-sufficient. The early pattern was of dispersed farms or small settlements in which the cultivated land area was small and in which woodland and other non-arable resources, often at a distance, were shared. When settlements were nucleated a bigger area of agricultural land was exploited and this also involved a reorganisation of land ownership. Rather later (from the early 10th century) came the 'great replanning' of both the lay-out of settlement and the open-fields. This took place in a landscape from which the small agricultural units had already been removed. All the basic conditions and the basic framework for the replanning of the landscape in the late Saxon period may therefore have been in place, including the major township boundaries. It has to be said that the creation of townships was not a single event. In some cases, as the place name *Newton* suggests (and there are three in the county) it could be a late Saxon or even a medieval phenomenon.

Brown and Foard note that 'The greatest mystery remains the character of the field systems associated with the Middle Saxon nucleated settlements'.[3] At present it looks as if the late Saxon replanning was so comprehensive that it swept away almost all trace of its predecessor. Probably this was because the landscape was pastoral in the Middle Saxon period and changed fundamentally when the open fields were laid out.

The background to the great replanning was almost certainly a rise in population and the development of an agricultural base able to support it. The need and desire to expand corn production was achieved by the creation of open fields in which the arable lands of the farmers were usually laid out in long narrow individual pieces grouped together in blocks called furlongs. That the whole thing was planned is shown by farmers being allotted lands in a sequence which could still be followed in later times. The introduction of the two- or three-field system was an ingenious way of enabling significant arable developments to take place while still maintaining a basic pastoral capacity. Significantly, the imposition of a new form of agricultural organisation fixed the settlement pattern at

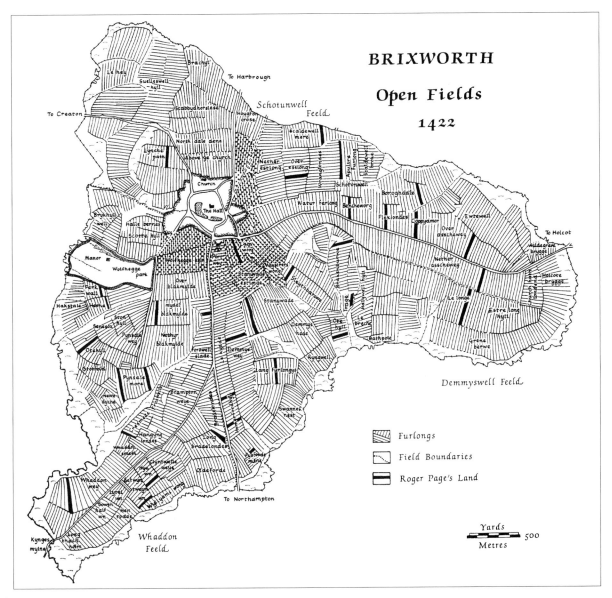

BRIXWORTH

Open Fields

1422

To Harbrough

To Creaton

Schotunwell Feeld

To Holcot

To Northampton

Whaddon Feeld

Demmyswell Feeld

Furlongs

Field Boundaries

Roger Page's Land

Yards
500
Metres

whatever level of nucleation it had reached, and controlled the basic form of subsequent development. In those places in Northamptonshire where woodland remained at the time of the great replanning, irregular field systems with dispersed settlement patterns are still to be found.

The growth of population and the development of agricultural production led to trade and the growth of a money economy. Urban life revived. Regional towns such as Northampton appeared, followed by lesser urban centres. By the time of the Conquest, Northamptonshire had five markets: Kings Sutton, Northampton, Higham Ferrers, Oundle and Peterborough, four of which were former soke centres.

23 *D.N. Hall's reconstruction of the open-fields of Brixworth as they were at their full extent, showing the arable lands and furlongs, together with meadows and slades. The lands in black are the yardland holdings of one farmer, Roger Page, dispersed in a sequence around the furlongs.*

One of the major objectives of the Great Replanning was the relating of the new agricultural system to the needs of royal taxation, whose later workings are recorded in Domesday Book, which sets out what each manor is assessed at in *hides*, the unit of taxation. In the case of Northamptonshire, historians have another, rather earlier Norman source, the Northamptonshire Geld Roll, which sets out the hidage assessments hundred by hundred, as they were at the end of the reign of Edward the Confessor.

The story of the great replanning is complicated by the fact that in the late ninth century Eastern England fell victim to the Danish invasions. The *Anglo-Saxon Chronicle* records a Viking foray in 869 which took them into East Anglia, where they martyred King Edmund and destroyed religious houses wherever they found them. 'They came to the monastery at Medeshamstede and burned and demolished it, reducing to nothing what had been a very rich foundation'. It was to lie waste for a century. In A.D. 873 Danish attacks led to the collapse of the kingdom of Mercia and the eventual partitioning of England between King Alfred and the Danes. The boundary they agreed cut the territory of Northamptonshire into two, the line marking the division being Watling Street.

In the Geld Roll there is a clear difference in the way that tax was levied between the south-west and the north-east of our area. In the south the standard of assessment for each hundred was 100 hides. In the north there was much irregularity of assessment, though the irregularities are less when it is seen that the north-east hundreds were grouped geographically in 'ship sokes'. This was the result of the reorganisation of local government after the re-conquest of Northamptonshire after the year 917.

Although Northamptonshire north and east of Watling Street fell under Danish rule for only four decades, changes other than in taxation took place. Danish farmers settled alongside the native English. Not surprisingly, they seem to have settled more heavily near to the Leicestershire and Lincolnshire borders, to the north of Northampton, in the Upper Ise valley, in Rockingham Forest and in the fens, rather than in the Nene Valley. They made Northampton the administrative capital of their territory and it seems odd that, in customary references to 'the Five Boroughs of the Danelaw', Northampton is never included as a sixth, as it surely was. Perhaps it was because it lay on the frontier rather than in the heartland of the Danelaw. The Danes created a defended borough at Northampton, as they had at Stamford, though they created towns for other purposes than defence. Despite their fierce reputation, the Danes were great traders and did much to foster commerce wherever they settled. They were, however, pagan. The bishopric of the Mercians was moved south from Leicester to the safety of Dorchester in the Thame Valley. What happened to the minsters and other churches of the area is not certain, because of extensive church rebuilding later, though it is likely they were destroyed. In the fabric of Brixworth there is evidence of damage by fire, which could date from these years.

I *The Archaeological excavation of the site cast of St Peter's church in Northampton was of national importance, revealing as it did the location of an earlier church, and the remains of two Middle-Saxon halls or 'palaces', the outline of which is where the workers are shown in the photograph.*

II *The great Saxon church of All Saints, Brixworth. It is believed that its fabric is still at the lower levels 7th-century and that here we have a church which takes us back to the origins of Anglo-Saxon christianity.*

24 *Strixton, enclosed about 1620, with lands and furlongs showing clearly in the large central field.*

In the early years of the 10th century the forces of the kings of Wessex began the re-conquest of the Danelaw. Alfred's son Edward the Elder and his thanes had learned the importance of fortifying urban places against the Danes, and the *Anglo-Saxon Chronicle* tells how, in 917, the fortifying of Towcester forced the Danes to lift their siege and retreat, and 'in the same autumn, King Edward went with the levies of Wessex to Passenham, and encamped there while the fortress at Towcester was being re-inforced by a stone wall. Jarl Thurfeth and the (Danish) barons submitted to him, together with the entire host ... which owed allegiance to Northampton, as far north as the Welland, and made submission to him as their lord and master'. The Wessex army repeated the process at Stamford, forcing submission by creating an English burh south of the river, which is still there in the form of the parish of St Martin's. Until late in the 20th century this remained in Northamptonshire, the main part of Stamford being in Lincolnshire across the Welland. The conquest of the Danelaw was completed by Aethelstan, the son of Edward the Elder, and his grandson, Edgar, became 'the first true king of England'.

Locally, the consequences were of long-lasting importance. As in other parts of re-conquered Mercia, a new county was created, based on the area which had owed allegiance to Danish Northampton, together with that part of 'free Northamptonshire' between Watling Street and Banbury, plus a portion of what later became Rutland across the Welland.

25 *The 11th-century tower of All Saints, Earls Barton, the most splendidly decorated surviving Saxon church tower in England.*

The first documentary reference to the county of Northampton is in 1011, though it may well nave been created earlier. Part of the reorganisation of government included the introduction of the land-related tax system recorded in Domesday Book of 1086, whereby hides are related to virgates, the farms of the peasants, using a terminology which historians still wrestle with today. There is no need to go into these complexities here, save to say that the system of calculation in the old Danelaw area was based on the Danish duodecimal system (4s., 8s., 12s.), whilst the part of the county which was outside Danish control was based on the Saxon decimal system, which indicates that the Danish part was hidated to fit in with the English part subsequent to the creation of the county.

The re-conquest of the pagan Danelaw led to a second great era of monasticism in the time of King Edgar (959-975). Prominent in this '10th-century reformation' were St Dunstan, archbishop of Canterbury and St Aethelwold, bishop of Winchester. After founding monasteries at Winchester and Ely, the latter came to Medeshamstede and caused a new religious house to be built which was eventually re-endowed with property on a generous scale. Early in the 11th century, the precinct was walled and became known as 'Burch' or 'Burgh'. When a flourishing town grew up outside its gates, it came to be called 'golden borough', and later Peterborough. Northamptonshire has a remarkable number of churches with features from this period of religious expansion, such as Earls Barton, Brigstock, Barnack and Stowe Nine Churches, with their fine towers, and Wittering, with its great chancel arch.

The re-conquest of the Danelaw did not mean the end of problems with Scandinavians. Raids began again in about 991 and Northamptonshire had to raise its share of Danegeld to buy them off. And it did not escape in the military and political troubles of the early 11th century. Northampton was burned in 1010, and again in 1065 by the Northumbrian and Welsh supporters of Earl Morcar, who had overthrown Tostig and marched south. Yet in spite of political instability, the 11th century was a time of considerable economic progress. This was not just happening in Northamptonshire, but in Lowland England as a whole. William the Conqueror knew he had acquired a rich land, and to find out how rich he caused the Domesday Survey to be made.

Domesday Book records the greatest upheaval the country had seen since the Danish conquest, or was to see again until the reign of Henry VIII. The English thanes, who in the century-and-a-half or so before the Battle of Hastings had emerged as feudal lords, were almost totally swept away and their manors passed to Normans, Frenchmen and Flemings. At the peak of the new feudal order was the king, possessed of some 59 manors and estates in Northamptonshire. Below him were his tenants-in-chief. First among these were the religious houses, the greatest of which was Peterborough Abbey, which retained its extensive estates after the Conquest. The religious houses were followed by churchmen, such as the Bishop of Bayeux and the Bishop of Coutances, who were rewarded with manors previously in the hands of English laymen. Then came the great lords, prominent amongst whom were the Count of Mortain and the Countess Judith, niece of the Conqueror and widow of the last Anglo-Saxon Earl of Northampton and Huntingdon. Her daughter married Simon de Senlis, who became the first Norman Earl of Northampton. Finally came the under-tenants, some of whom, like William Peverel, Scott's 'Peveril of the Peak', were considerable lords in their own right with manors in several counties, and a few, mostly Normans who held by serjeanty and Englishmen styled 'the king's thanes', had more modest fiefs.

26 *Early Norman font, Little Billing.*

The Norman take-over was not trouble-free, as the case of Peterborough Abbey illustrates. Its patriotic abbot, Leofric, died at Hastings, and Brand, his elected successor, accepted investiture at the hand of Edgar the Aetheling, which brought down the wrath of King William on his head, and it cost him 40 marcs of gold (£240) for reconciliation. In 1069 Brand died and William took the opportunity to appoint a Norman warrior-monk, Turold, abbot. It was to be his role to guard the abbey from attack by Hereward the Wake and his outlaws from the Fens. Before Turold even arrived, 'Hereward and his gang' struck. When the new abbot got to Peterborough he found it burned to the ground and the monks scattered. The buildings were restored, but knights to serve the abbot had to be provided for. From then on William made the monastery liable for the cost of finding 60 knights. Devout as the Conqueror was, his hand lay as heavy on Peterborough as it did on the rest of Northamptonshire.

2

Medieval Northamptonshire

Domesday Book and After

Domesday Book is the most remarkable document of its time. Drawn up as an inventory of the wealth of England, it illuminates medieval society as no survey before or after does. However, it records English society at an arbitrary point in time fixed by politics. The year 1086 was not the beginning or end of any social or economic trend, or phase of development. It has been said England was 'an old country' by 1086: the settlement of the landscape had been going forward for about five centuries, but the peak of the medieval expansion was not to be reached for another two.

27 *Wooden effigies of a knight and a lady, St Mary, Woodford. They are believed to be Sir Walter Traylli and Alianore, his wife.*

By 1086 all the first- and second-quality land in Northamptonshire had been settled and already the acreage of land under the plough was probably greater than at the height of English arable farming in the 19th century. The number of villages (some 326) recorded in Domesday Book is about the same as today, though a few, which appear in charters of the pre-Conquest period, are unrecorded or not recorded separately. Similarly, some forty modern villages are not mentioned, these being settled after 1086. From the number of people and plough-teams per square mile recorded in the Survey the most thickly-peopled area was the Nene Valley, especially between Irthlingborough and Fotheringhay to this day the most fertile farming area. The most thinly-settled areas lay in the woodlands of Rockingham, Salcey and Whittlewood, in the fen around Peterborough, and around Guilsborough on the colder soils of the Northampton Heights.

Domesday Book portrays Northamptonshire as a rich and fertile country fast recovering from the depredations of the 1060s. After extensive re-stocking, the values of the manors had recovered: only one place was still completely waste, though there were waste holdings in 13 others, and a number of waste houses in Northampton. However, in the Nene Valley values had doubled since 1066, and in the Peterborough district they had increased four-fold. Many entries record the existence of valuable meadowland. As might be expected, it was most heavily concentrated in the valleys of the Nene and the Ise. There are also a number of references to woodland, most of which correspond to the later forests of Rockingham, Whittlewood and Salcey and their margins. The survey also mentions ironworks at Corby and Gretton, and the presence of smiths at Deene, Greens Norton and Towcester, all in, or near to, the woodland sources of charcoal. By 1086 it is clear that water-power was extensively used in Northamptonshire. One hundred and fifty-five manors had a water-mill, and three—Finedon, Harrington and Evenley—had four each. Sometimes associated with them were fisheries, and seven of the manors in the Nene Valley below Irthlingborough rendered eels in considerable quantities to their lords as manorial dues.

Domesday Book mentions the existence of markets at Higham Ferrers, Kings Sutton and Oundle, though there must surely have been others, Northampton and Peterborough being the most obvious omissions.

28 *Barnwell Mill.*

29 *Rockingham Castle, drawn by George Clarke of Scaldwell, about 1842.*

30 *The Bocase Stone in Harry's Wood, near Brigstock, is a memorial on the site of an ancient oak—the Bocase Tree. No one is sure what the significance of the Bocase Tree was. It may well have been an old traditional forest meeting place but, whatever it was, when it succumbed to old age in the 17th century it was thought fit to mark the place where it once stood.*

31 *Helpston church and medieval market cross.*

Northampton is the only place where burgesses are recorded, indicating that in 1086 it was the only borough in Northamptonshire. The presence of only one castle is recorded, at Rockingham, which 'was waste when King William ordered a castle to be made there', adding 'it is now worth 26 shillings'. The great castle at Northampton was built just after. Only three churches are mentioned, but some 61 priests connected with 60 manors are listed.

In this fertile landscape the extension of population, land under the plough, and settlements was to go on apace, reaching its peak about the year 1300. By then, according to one estimate, the population had grown from about 30,000 at the time of Domesday book to a peak of about 104,000, and it is worth comparing this latter figure with that for the county at the time of the first census in 1801— 132,000. The decline that set in during the 14th century was undoubtedly severe and prolonged. By the time of the Poll Tax of 1377 it has been estimated that it had fallen by as much as 40 per cent under the impact of a series of epidemics, the most severe of which was the visitation of the Bubonic plague ('The Black Death') of 1348-50.

At the time of Domesday Book there was still plenty of uncultivated land and tracts of woodland where hunting had been enjoyed since at least as early as Roman times. Yet the survey makes only one reference to woodland being 'in the King's forest'. Under the succeeding Norman and Angevin kings the area of the county brought under royal forest law increased spectacularly. Eventually a line of royal hunting lodges from Silverstone in the south to Kings Cliffe in the north was built to which the king and his friends retired for the enjoyment of the chase. By the time of the Perambulation of 1286 about half of the county had been brought into the royal forest. However, from that time baronial pressure compelled Edward I to accept new, and smaller, boundaries which severely limited the extent of the county under the jurisdiction of the royal forest courts.

Such pressure undoubtedly came as one result of the land-hunger occasioned by the expansion of population and settlement in the two centuries since Domesday Book. Certainly by 1300 all the marginal land had been settled. In this period more than half of the new settlements

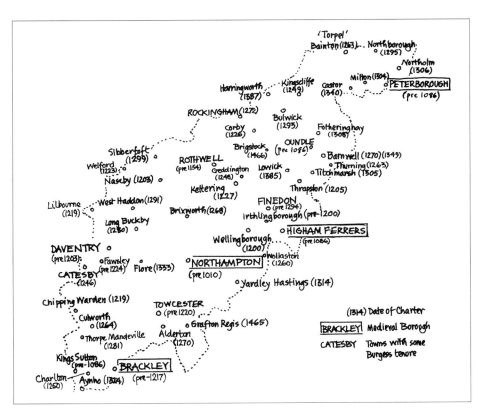

32 *The 49 places in the county with market charters in the medieval era. No more than a third survived as markets after 1500.*

were in the fen around Peterborough, and other villages appear in the woodland districts where, from the early 12th century, assarting had gone on extensively. In the older, richer, fielden areas villages grew larger, developing 'cotten ends' and hiving off hamlets. By about 1300 there were roughly 350 villages and hamlets in the shire.

One result of the continuous expansion of the period between Domesday Book and 1300 was an extension of the network of trade and exchange. Charters obtained by their manorial lords made a remarkable number of villages into little market towns, particularly in the 13th century. Most did not survive the great contraction after 1350 as markets, though in villages such as Chipping (*i.e.*, Market) Warden, Naseby, Helpston and many others the stumps and steps of market crosses, and the sites of former market places, can still be seen to this day. In the years before 1300 some market towns were granted borough charters: Northampton receiving its first in 1189, Brackley in 1235 and Higham Ferrers in 1251. In addition to these,

33 *What was once the market place of Brigstock. The date of its charter was 1466. Although the royal hunting lodge had been long gone, the king's tenants were given a market. The market cross is Elizabethan and the grant was renewed in 1604 'for the support and relief of the poor inhabitants of the said town'.*

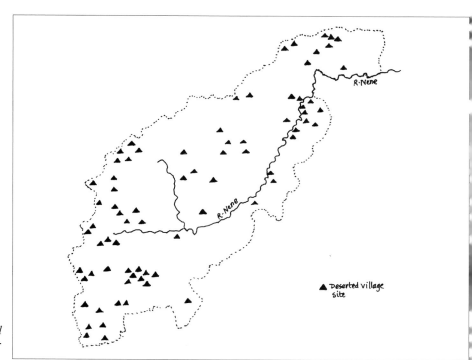

34 *Deserted medieval villages in Northampton-shire.*

35 *Knutcote, at the south end of Naseby, showing the sites of deserted house platforms, sunken ways and possibly small fish ponds. This low-lying end of the village was probably depopulated in the 15th century. Since this photograph was taken, in about 1970, this part of the village has seen a fair amount of house-building.*

another 12 places have been listed as having some burgage tenure, usually taken as a sign of 'borough' or near-borough status. Not one of the other towns, however, remotely rivalled Northampton in size and importance, and the medieval history of the county capital will be examined in a section of its own.

By the beginning of the 14th century it is clear that over-population and over-cropping were starting to cause problems. In the succeeding two centuries there followed a prolonged sequence of harvest failures and famines which in turn exposed the population to epidemics and outbreaks of pestilence. There is also some evidence that there was a worsening of the climate in the 14th century. The long-term result was a marked contraction of population, land under the plough, and economic activity. One feature of this is the shrinkage of many settlements and the complete abandonment of a number of other hamlets and villages. In Northamptonshire more than eighty examples of 'Deserted Medieval Villages' have been recorded, and the depopulation of a great proportion of these took place between 1350 and 1500. In 1356 it was recorded 'no one dwells or has dwelt in Hale [in Apethorpe] since the pestilence and the land is wasted by the king's deer'.[4] A number were hamlets on exposed or poor soil on which it had perhaps always been hard to scrape a living; a number, however, were deserted as the result of population shrinkage combined with a new development in farming which emerged in the 15th century—large-scale sheep grazing. Another cause of depopulated villages was the emparking of manor houses by the new gentry of the 15th and 16th centuries.

The general reduction in economic activity resulted in a lessening in the trade in agricultural produce which led to the decline of many market towns. Some reverted to being mere villages, and others underwent a long period of stagnation. It was not until the reign of Queen Elizabeth I that population growth and the recovery of inland trade began to revitalise some of them. However, the new pattern of trade was in some respects different from that of medieval England, and many never revived as market towns. The social consequences of late medieval population decline and village desertion were not all unfortunate. Under the changed conditions of life in the countryside in the 14th and 15th centuries the feudal system disintegrated. Now labour was scarcer manorial lords were prepared to convert feudal services into money payments, and were prepared to convert feudal tenures into leasehold and copyhold. With more land to go round, these centuries were looked back on as something of a golden age for peasant and cottager alike, though to remember it this way the famines, pestilences and wars needed to be put out of mind.

Medieval Northampton

Because of its strategic position 'in the middle of the kingdom', situated on one of the great roads to the north, Northampton was deliberately

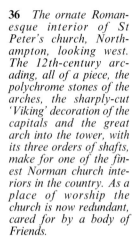

36 *The ornate Romanesque interior of St Peter's church, Northampton, looking west. The 12th-century arcading, all of a piece, the polychrome stones of the arches, the sharply-cut 'Viking' decoration of the capitals and the great arch into the tower, with its three orders of shafts, make for one of the finest Norman church interiors in the country. As a place of worship the church is now redundant, cared for by a body of Friends.*

expanded by the Normans after the Conquest. By the time of the Domesday Survey in 1086 a 'new borough' had been added to the existing one, the town growing first to the north of the Mayorhold outside the old North Gate, and later to the east of the 'English' town. Judged by its walled area, medieval Northampton was the third largest town in the country after London and Norwich. For the next century Northampton's fortunes were presided over by three Norman Earls of Northampton, father, son and grandson, all called Simon de Senlis, all active in the promotion of their borough. The first and greatest of these earls built the castle to guard West Bridge (and overawe the town), probably built the town wall, and founded the Priory of St Andrew and the churches of the Holy Sepulchre and All Saints as well. Tradition also has it that he was the builder of South Bridge *(c.*1100). Simon II was a great patron of religion and was the founder of Delapré Nunnery, just south of the town, and it was Simon III who was probably the rebuilder of St Peter's church in the late 12th century.

However, even before 1185, when the earldom of Northampton became extinct on the death of Simon III, the castle had been taken over by the Crown, and for the next two hundred years or so, because of its strategic position and of the peripatetic character of the medieval monarchy, Northampton was a place where great events of state took place. It was important in times of civil war; in 1215 the first move of the barons against King John was to lay siege to it, and in 1264 a great battle between the Royalists and Simon de Montfort was fought nearby. Northampton Castle was a venue of both business and pleasure for the Angevin kings. It was used as a hunting lodge, and a royal deer park was made nearby at Moulton for the king to hunt in when at Northampton. Between 1200 and 1377 the castle was the setting for a number of tournaments. Great councils of the realm and parliaments were held there in the 12th and 13th centuries, and no less than three crusades were proclaimed in Northampton. Perhaps the most momentous event was the condemnation of Thomas à Becket in 1164. Northampton reached its apogee as a town of national renown about the time of the Great Pestilence in 1348. The parliament of 1380 was the last to assemble there, and the final event of national significance was in 1460, when Warwick the Kingmaker overthrew Henry VI after a battle in the

37 *Medieval mayor's seal.*

meadows between the river and
Delapré Nunnery.

The rise of Northampton to
prominence saw important extensions
to its privileges. From about 1283 it
returned two burgesses to parliament, as befitted a borough which
by then had already extracted measures of self-government from the
Crown. The extinction of the earldom upon the death of Simon de
Senlis III had given Northampton the
chance to negotiate directly with the
king. In a series of charters starting

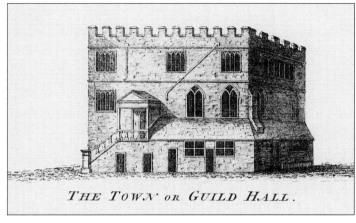

THE TOWN OR GUILD HALL.

in 1189 the burgesses progressively secured more control over their own
affairs, and by the end of the Middle Ages the government of the town
was vested in a Mayor and Corporation whose powers were confirmed
in an Act of Parliament of 1489. This process was, however, accompanied by a struggle for power in the town between a rich oligarchy and
the popular element. By the 15th century the town assembly had been
superseded by the Mayor and Corporation, who now had the power to
nominate new members of the Corporation, who stayed in office for life.
Government by 'close corporation' lasted virtually unchanged until 1835.

These rights of self-government were such that any town which rose
to the economic importance of Northampton would aspire to. In the 11th
century it ranked about twentieth among English towns. By the mid-12th
century it had risen to about sixth place. It has never been as prominent,
nationally, since. In common with many other provincial towns in the
Middle Ages it reached its peak about the year 1300. By then its population was about 3,700, compared with just over 1,000 at the time of
Domesday Book. However, by 1377, it had dropped to about 2,000. A
hundred and fifty years later, in 1524, the population had still not recovered to the figure for 1300: it then stood at between 2,800 and 3,000. In
the later Middle Ages, then, Northampton underwent a long period of
decline.

The wealth of medieval Northampton rested on its weekly markets,
its annual fairs, and the produce of its network of crafts. Northampton
was never merely a local market town, but was a flourishing county
capital whose annual cycle of fairs attracted trade from a wide area. At
the peak of its medieval prosperity there were five of these, by far the
greatest of which was St Hugh's in November, which almost certainly
had originated before the Conquest. At its peak in the 14th century it
lasted the whole month of November, and ranked alongside Boston,
Winchester, St Ives, and Stourbridge in Cambridgeshire as one of the
great international fairs of Medieval England. Fair, market, and traverse-
tolls were an important source of borough revenue in this period—the
latter being collected as far away as 15 miles from the town.

38 *The 15th-century
Guildhall of Northamp-
ton, which stood on the
corner of Wood Hill and
Abington Street. It
housed the town's local
government until the early
1860s, when it was
replaced by a new
Guildhall (see plate 172),
and demolished.*

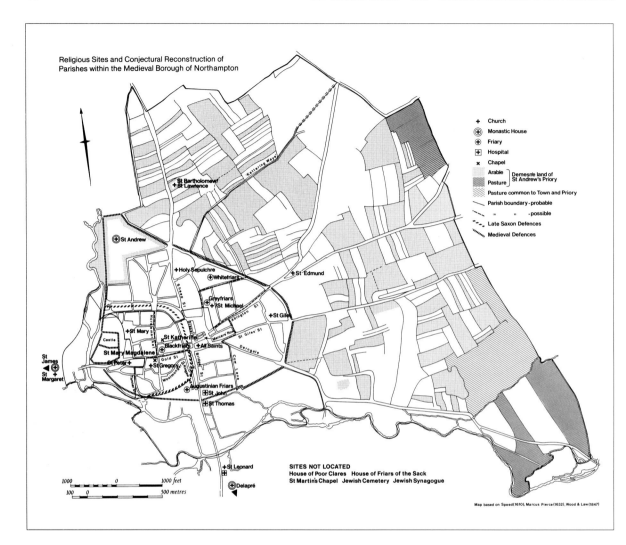

Religious Sites and Conjectural Reconstruction of
Parishes within the Medieval Borough of Northampton

+   Church
⊕   Monastic House
⊕   Friary
⊞   Hospital
×   Chapel
         Arable ⎤ Demesne land of
         Pasture ⎦ St Andrew's Priory
         Pasture common to Town and Priory
         Parish boundary - probable
         "   "   - possible
         Late Saxon Defences
         Medieval Defences

SITES NOT LOCATED
House of Poor Clares   House of Friars of the Sack
St Martin's Chapel   Jewish Cemetery   Jewish Synagogue

Map based on Speed (1610), Marcus Pierce (1632), Wood & Law (1847)

39 *Medieval Northampton, its religious institutions and fields, based on Marcus Pierce's 'a True Plot and description of al the Ancient Demesne Lands belonginge to the Priorye of St Andrews', 1632. The very extensive holdings of St Andrew's should be noted. (See also colour plate VII, facing p.80.)*

Much of Northampton's wealth stemmed from its crafts. It was a great centre of cloth-weaving and dyeing: in 1334 there were said to be '300 workers of cloths', and a strong local tradition maintains that it was a place where London cloth was sent to be dyed. From about that time the trade began to decline when there was a general move of the cloth industry from the towns into the countryside. But the decline of Northampton's trade was slow and prolonged: as late as 1524 clothworkers were still the second largest group among the town's crafts. However, the trade did not re-establish itself in the county in the 16th century, despite the fact that by this period Northamptonshire had become a notable wool-producing area. Another Northampton speciality was tanning and leather-working, which may well have originally been stimulated by the presence of the royal court at the castle as well as by the plentiful local supplies of oak

40 *Northampton market place today. Still a great open space with moveable stalls, it is one of the sights of England.*

bark for tanning and leather. As cloth-working declined the leather trades became more prominent: by 1524 leather workers had become the largest single group of craftsmen in the town and, amongst them, the shoemakers were the most numerous. Northampton's specialisation in footwear, therefore, goes back at least to the reign of Henry VIII and probably much earlier. Other medieval trades included ironworking and victualling, for the markets of Northampton were great suppliers of provisions, as they are today.

Until the 15th century there are no references to craft gilds or organisations in Northampton. However, the *Liber Custumarum*—the book of the customs of Northampton—records the setting up of craft and livery companies for tailors, shoemakers, weavers, fullers and others from about 1430. It is clear that the borough corporation was keeping a tight control of the crafts, restricting entry into them to 'freemen', and insisting that the trades should divide the market, keep out strangers, and regulate their apprentices and journeymen. These companies ruled the town trades down to the middle of the 17th century.

From the early 14th century there were many and frequent complaints of the decay of Northampton. No doubt some of these were aimed at reducing the tax burden, and no doubt some of the decay within the town walls may have been caused by people moving into 'suburbs' outside the gates. However, there seems little doubt that in the 14th, 15th and 16th centuries the town was in decline as a result of the fall in population and reduction in inland trade in the later Middle Ages, and

41 *Rose window and seal of St John's hospital.*

42   Perpendicular tower of Whiston.

the consequent decline of markets, fairs, and the urban cloth trade. Northampton's recovery did not really start until the time of Queen Elizabeth I.

Religion in Medieval Northamptonshire

Northamptonshire is deservedly famous for its medieval churches. It possesses examples of each of the medieval styles of church architecture as fine as any in England: St Peter's, Northampton and Castor in the Norman; Warmington and Higham Ferrers in the Early English; Cotterstock in the Decorated; Lowick and Fotheringhay in the Perpendicular. Yet, as might be expected from its economic history, the county is richer in churches in the first three of these styles, built from about 1190 to 1360, than it is in the last, dating from between 1360 and about 1530. Despite Titchmarsh, Whiston and the retro-choir at Peterborough, it does not have a range of rebuilt Perpendicular churches to compare with East Anglia, Gloucestershire or Somerset. Perhaps if it had become a centre of the late medieval cloth industry, as well as a great wool-growing county, the story might have been different.

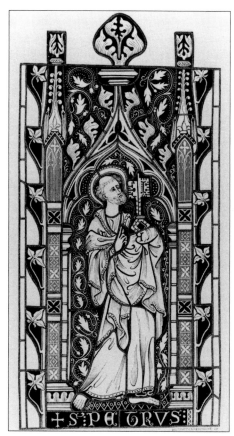

43   An image of St Peter in stained glass in the church of St Nicholas, Stanford on Avon, which possesses one of the finest sets of 14th-century glass in England.

Splendid though many of its parish churches are, they have come down to us as mere shells of what they were before the Reformation and the Civil War. Except for the survival of a few remnants of medieval stained-glass, wall-paintings, rood screens and college stalls, many of the physical expressions in them of the piety of medieval people have long gone. In particular, the details of the altars, images and lights to be found in even the smallest parish church can only be recovered, imperfectly, from documentary evidence such as late medieval wills. The life of the people was integrated into a yearly cycle of religious festivals and rituals in a way that was never the same after the Reformation. For example, the first rule of the ordinances of the weavers' craft in Northampton in 1432 laid it down that the masters and journeymen of the trade were, as a preliminary to their annual feast, to process every Easter Monday with tapers of wax 'as it hath been continued of Ancient time' to the nunnery of St Mary de la Pré beside Northampton, there to offer the tapers up to the images of the Trinity and Our Lady.

Most parish churches were built, rebuilt and furnished by the local community, whose individual members usually remain anonymous. Some churches, however, received the special patronage of the rich and mighty, and their visual splendour reflects this. The magnificence of the tower and west porch of Higham Ferrers reflects the patronage of the mighty Earls of Lancaster, into whose hands the manor passed in 1266. This was enhanced in the 15th century through the benefactions of Higham's most famous son, Henry Chichele, founder of All Souls College, Oxford, and Archbishop of Canterbury. In his native town he founded a college and furnished the choir in the parish church to accommodate its members. Within the churchyard he endowed a chantry (or school) and left a bequest to found a Bede House to accommodate 12 men of the parish in their old age. The setting of the church, churchyard and its other foundations makes Higham the finest monument to the Middle Ages in the county. Higham was first made splendid by the House of Lancaster: Fotheringhay was the work of Edmund of Langley, fifth son of Edward III and founder of the powerful House of York. He, too, founded a college there and began a magnificent collegiate church, which his descendants turned into the mausoleum of the House of York.

44 *The church of St Mary, Higham Ferrers, with its superb west doorway and crocketed spire, Archbishop Chichele's school on the left, and part of the Bede House visible on the right.*

In the scale of things in the medieval church the parish and its priest ranked rather low. At the top was the monastic ideal, greater in Norman and Angevin times than in Saxon. At the time of the Conquest there was only one monastery in the county—the great house at Peterborough, refounded about the year 966. Peterborough, magnificently rebuilt in the 12th century, always remained far and away the greatest of the Northamptonshire religious foundations and was one of the dozen wealthiest monasteries in medieval England. Two more religious houses were founded

45 *Portrait of Archbishop Chichele.*

in the early Norman period, the abbeys of St Andrew and St James, both at Northampton. In the next century, an age of religious revival, another 11 were added, followed by six in the 13th century. Some idea of their relative wealth and standing can be gleaned from their valuation in Henry VIII's *Valor Ecclesiasticus* of 1535. The Benedictine abbey of Peterborough was six times as valuable as the next richest house, the Cistercian foundation at Pipewell. Assessed at about the same as Pipewell were the Cluniac House of St Andrew, Northampton, the Premonstratensian house of Sulby and the house of the Austin Canons, St James, Northampton. Next came the nunneries at Catesby and Delapré, and the priory of Canons Ashby. These were followed

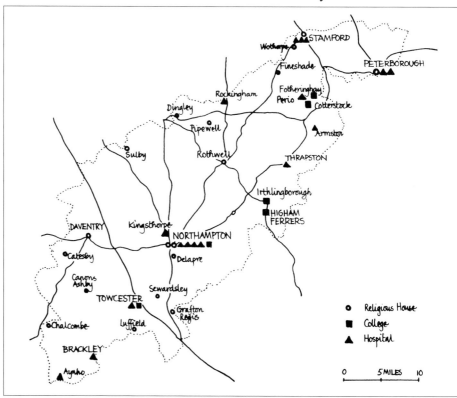

46 *The principal monasteries, nunneries and other religious foundations of medieval Northamptonshire. The priories of Luffield and Daventry were dissolved before the Reformation.*

47 *The great church of St Mary and All Saints, Fotheringhay, close by the castle. Splendid though it is, it is but a shell of what it once was. Built after 1434 in the Perpendicular style, it was intended to be a shrine to the Yorkist dynasty, and it had a college attached to it. The Yorkist dynasty fell, and at the Reformation the college and the chancel were demolished and with them the monuments to the House of York. Virtually nothing of the heraldic glass or other fittings survived, except a fine pulpit.*

by three smaller houses, Chalcombe Priory, St Michael at Stamford, and the house of the Austin Canons at Fineshade. Lowest in value came two small nunneries at Sewardsley and Rothwell.

As well as representing the highest form of the medieval ideal of the devout and holy life, the religious houses played an increasingly important part in the economic life of the county as the Middle Ages wore on. Often endowed at their foundation with lands and parish rectories, in the course of time bequests to them by the faithful increased their wealth and property. Some of this was turned to religious uses; their convent churches were rebuilt, sometimes on an impressive scale. They acquired relics,

48 *Pinnacle of the middle gable of the west front of Peterborough Cathedral.*

pilgrimages to the shrines of which were made by the devout and the sick, the most venerated locally being the arm of St Oswald at Peterborough and the finger of St Andrew at St Andrew's, Northampton. Much of their wealth, however, went into economic enterprise. The abbey stewards often managed considerable estates, and some in the 12th and 13th centuries were involved in the draining of the fens, and planting granges in newly-tamed and colonised woodland areas.

The inevitable worldliness that accompanied the accumulation of wealth was one reason at least for the new versions of the monastic rule that appeared in the Middle Ages. Benedictine was followed by Cluniac, Augustinian by Cistercian and Premonstratensian. In the 13th century the friars, whose task it was to evangelise the poor of the towns, appeared, and Northampton became one of the 11 towns in England in which all four orders of mendicants established themselves. In addition to the monasteries, nunneries and friaries, some 18 hospitals were founded in Northamptonshire, as well as a hermitage at Grafton Regis and a house of the Knights Hospitaller at Dingley. In the later Middle Ages, so numerous had monastic foundations become, that the devout sought other channels for their pious bequests, and the practice grew up of founding chantries in parish churches and endowing priests to say masses for the souls of the dead. By the early 16th century there were 30 in Northamptonshire.

Another late medieval religious development was the founding of collegiate institutions whose functions included acting as a chantry for the souls of the benefactors, a college for mass-priests and choristers, a religious school, and, sometimes, a place of care for the aged. The common practice was to allot the chancel of the parish church to the college, the nave remaining congregational under a vicar. Starting in 1339 with Cotterstock, by 1460 there were six colleges in the county; the others being at Higham Ferrers, Fotheringhay, Towcester, Irthlingborough, and All Saints, Northampton.

49 *Common seal of the Abbey of St James, 'extra Northampton'.*

It would, however, be wrong to believe that religious feeling in the Middle Ages was always constant and orthodox. Amongst both clergy and layfolk it was liable to ebb and flow. Reformed monastic orders and

50 *The former hospital of St James and St John, Brackley. Restored in the 19th century, it became the chapel of Magdalen College School.*

51 *The Eleanor Cross, Hardingstone, Northampton, erected by Edward I in 1291 to mark one of the resting places (Delapre Abbey) of his wife's funeral cortège on its journey from Lincolnshire to London after her death. Only three of these crosses survive, two in Northamptonshire.*

evangelical enterprises emerged periodically to revitalise it. And there were reactions to these efforts as observance, both within and without the religious houses, grew lax or anti-clericalism began to spread. In the late 14th century Northampton became a centre of Lollardy and at least one mayor gave strong and open support to Lollard preachers. A century later episcopal visitations uncovered evidence of laxness and indulgence in the sins of the flesh in several of the religious houses. More disturbing, perhaps, there was evidence of a decline in the numbers of religious: in 1488 there were only four priests, one deacon and two novices in the Abbey of Sulby, in addition to the abbot and sub-prior. Nevertheless, by the early years of the reign of Henry VIII so old and so much part of the fabric of the life of the community had the monasteries, nunneries, friaries, colleges and chantries become, that people could hardly have expected that, within the space of a very few years, all would be swept away.

52 *Conventual seal of Catesby Priory, dedicated to the Virgin and St Edmund.*

3

Tudor and Stuart Northamptonshire

The Reformation

After failing to obtain a papal annulment of his marriage to Katherine of Aragon, Henry VIII began his onslaught on the Catholic church in 1534 with the Act of Supremacy. In the following year the first effects began to be felt in Northamptonshire when Thomas Cromwell's commissioners made their visitation to the principal monasteries, nunneries and friaries. Within the space of five years all had been closed, their contents dispersed, their buildings and lands sold. Within 20 years the endowments of the chantries and colleges had been appropriated, the property of the religious guilds confiscated, and the endowments, vestments, images, altars, and lights of the parish churches had been seized. By 1553 the church had been effectively de-Romanised.

There were, in fact, two inquiries into the religious houses of the county, one by Cromwell's agents, the other by local gentlemen. Of the two, the first was the more anti-monastic, though its members, looking for evidence of evils and abuses, were hard pressed to find many. On the whole the religious houses were given good reports: the monks and nuns were living devout and holy lives; the poor friars really were poor; the religious houses were generous almsgivers. The local gentlemen were more sympathetic and pleaded for exceptions to be made in the general suppression. 'When the visitors were lately in these parts they visited the monastery at Pipewell, where the abbot and his brethren obeyed the injunctions. But this house being of very small revenue, keeping continual hospitality, relieving the poor, maintaining divine service in as virtuous and laudable a manner as any I know ... I beg you will have pity on them in this behalf, and grant them a disposition at my request', wrote Sir William Parr of Horton.[5]

The king and Cromwell allowed no pleas and no exemptions: the religious houses were closed and their property confiscated. The monks and nuns negotiated for, and received, pensions, and the moveable wealth of the monasteries passed to the Crown, as did their land, which soon came on to the market. The Dissolution saw, in fact, the greatest redistribution of wealth since 1066: as much as a quarter of the total wealth of the country changed hands. It has been estimated that half to two-thirds of the wealth of the monasteries in Northamptonshire found its way into the hands of local men. In this buyers' market William Parr was the chief beneficiary: others who did well included the elder Sir Thomas Tresham ('Prior Tresham') who received much of the land of Pipewell; Sir Edward Griffin, who acquired the house and land of the Knights Hospitaller at Dingley; and the Brudenells, who bought up much of the land of Fineshade. Interestingly, the latter three were families later to be strongly Catholic: at the time of the Dissolution their religion proved no bar to the acquisition of monastic property. Greed played a notable part in the whole exercise. 'At Delapray I had 2 chalices and a pyx, and the house was greatly stored with cattle and corn. You shall see me make you a pretty bank by the time I come up next', wrote Cromwell's servant, the odious Dr. London.[6] At the Dissolution of Pipewell the commissioners resorted to a practice fairly generally indulged in: while the abbey seal was still valid the monks were persuaded or bullied into granting annuities to the spoilsmen. Edward Montagu, John Montagu, William Saunders, George Gifford and 13 others helped themselves in this way.

53 *Effigy in Rushton church of Sir Thomas Tresham (died 1559), robed as the last Prior of the Order of St John of Jerusalem in England, re-established by Queen Mary.*

The Northamptonshire houses wisely surrendered without resistance, and violence was not used upon them. In depressed Northampton there was regret at their passing; the townspeople unsuccessfully petitioned the king to spare the Abbey of St James, which was generous to the poor. Later, in the reign of Philip and Mary, they requested Cardinal Pole to restore the abbey— a very rare thing indeed. However, there was no major public indignation at the Dissolution, though things may have been different if the Pilgrimage of Grace had spread from Lincolnshire. The decay of the town of Northampton was visibly added to by the running down of monastic property and the closing of the now

54 *The church of St Mary, Canon's Ashby. All that remains of the Augustinian Priory founded there c.1150.*

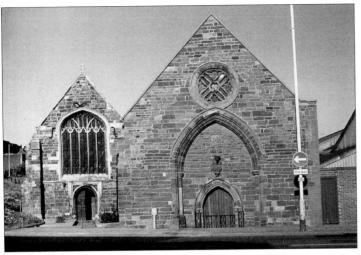

55 *St John's Hospital, Northampton. It was in danger of demolition as a result of railway activity in the 1870s, but was saved and for some years was a Catholic church. More recently it had various uses, including one as a Bierkeller. Currently empty, its future is again in doubt.*

56 *Part of the medieval cloister of Peterborough Abbey.*

'redundant' religious houses and their chapels. The number of churches was reduced to the four ancient parish churches of the centre of the town—St Peter's, Holy Sepulchre, St Giles' and All Saints. The hospitals fell into decline, though they were not all closed, and the subsequent history of certain of them is unsavoury. The mastership of the hospital of St John the Baptist in Northampton, for instance, became a lucrative sinecure in the gift of the bishop of London, and as early as 1584 it was said that hardly a twentieth part of the revenues were given to the relief of any aged or feeble persons.

Between the Dissolution of the religious houses and the accession of Queen Mary the Reformation proceeded apace. The monastery of Peterborough was dissolved, but the church and its precinct were preserved: the king had a use for them. In 1541 he hived off Northamptonshire and Rutland from the great medieval see of Lincoln and made Peterborough the cathedral of this new diocese. The last abbot, John Chambers, who 'loved to sleep in a whole skin, and desired to die in his nest wherein he had lived so long'[7] became the first bishop, and the last prior of St Andrew's, Northampton, became the first dean. On the Dissolution, the king made a tripartite division of the rich revenues of the monastery, assigning a third to himself, a third to the new bishop, and the remainder to the dean and chapter. The old territorial domain of the abbey was given the status of a soke, or liberty, whose civil government was vested in the lord of the hundred (passing into the hands of the Cecils in 1576), in a *custos rotulorum* and magistrates appointed by the Crown, and in the high bailiff of the city, who was appointed by the dean and chapter of the cathedral, who were lords of the manor. More sourly, Peterborough became known as 'the least city and poorest bishopric in England'.

At the same time the process of secularising the parish started. In many the rectorial rights and advowson passed from the religious

houses to laymen, principally the local gentry. In the reign of Edward VI the medieval altars, images and lights and rood screens were removed, and wall paintings whitewashed over. The 30 Northamptonshire chantries were suppressed, and endowments for stipendiary priests, employed to say masses for the dead, were seized, weakening the endowments of many a rectory and vicarage. The colleges attached to parish churches in such places as Fotheringhay, Irthlingborough, and Higham Ferrers were dissolved, and the property of religious guilds confiscated. In 1552 there was a massive final confiscation of parish property: vestments, sacred vessels and ornaments were seized. The plunder was not used for any religious or national purpose.

The apparently passive way Northamptonshire accepted religious change from above was repeated when Queen Mary came to the throne and restored Catholicism as the religion of England. The clergy accepted the restoration of the Old Faith rather more easily than elsewhere—only one in 10 being deprived of their livings for consciences' sake against a national pattern of one in five. And the laity obeyed the queen, one solitary Protestant being burned for heresy, John Kurde, a shoemaker from Syresham. The queen, however, did not live long enough to undo the work of her father and brother, for within five years she was dead.

When Queen Elizabeth succeeded in 1558 there was once more a decided shift away from Rome, though at first the queen moved cautiously. Sixteen Northampton priests were deprived of their livings;

57 *Irthlingborough church and the tower of the former medieval college, in an engraving of 1846.*

58 *The burning of John Kurde, a Syresham shoemaker, for heresy in the time of Queen Mary. The engraving is from Foxe's* Acts and Monuments, *which did so much to foster English hostility to Catholicism.*

59 *Abbot's tombstone from Sulby.*

Bishop Pole of Peterborough, Chambers' Catholic successor, was ejected; and so was the dean. The next year the queen imposed a general religious settlement, resistance to which did not appear immediately. However, in the following generation both Catholic and the Puritan reaction to it in Northamptonshire were to be notable.

Economic Change: Enclosure, Sheep-farming and Wayfaring

In June 1607 the peace of Northamptonshire was disturbed by a peasant uprising that was of more than local significance. At Newton, near Kettering, about a thousand armed people set about tearing up the hedges with which Squire Tresham had enclosed the open-field arable land on his estate. They styled themselves 'levellers' and were led by one John Reynolds, who called himself 'Captain Pouch', because of a great leather pouch which he wore by his side, in which purse, he told his followers, 'there was sufficient matter to defend them against all comers'.[8] What these 'levellers' were taking direct action against was a process that had been going on for about 150 years or so in the Midlands—the enclosing of arable land for sheep pasture, a process often accompanied by deliberate depopulation by landlords. It was hated by the cottagers and peasantry; parsons preached against it from the pulpit; and resistance to it was capable of alarming the government.

In the event, Pouch's rising was suppressed by the local Justices of the Peace, using their armed tenants. After a sharp fight the levellers were routed and some who were taken prisoner were afterwards hanged and quartered, their quarters being set up at Northampton, Oundle, Thrapston, and other places, as a warning. Pouch's purse was found to contain nothing more than a piece of green cheese. The incident was one of a number at that time in the counties of Oxford, Warwick and Northampton, and so alarmed the government that a Commission to Inquire into Depopulation was set up (as had been done in 1517). But although statutes were passed against depopulation, and depopulating landlords occasionally fined, it all had little, if any, effect. The process went forward throughout the 17th century in a piecemeal way (as it had in the 16th) and the spread of permanent pasture for cattle grazing and for sheepwalks increased steadily in Northamptonshire. The county became renowned for the quantity and fineness of the wool it produced. By 1800 it is estimated that, with its 640,000 sheep, it was, after Lincolnshire, the second largest producer of long wool in England.

Most of the wool was always sent out of the county to be manufactured elsewhere. As John Morton noted about 1712:

A great Part of our Pasture-Wooll [i.e., long-haired wool] is bought up by Factors, and convey'd to Stourbridge-Fair, and thence to *Norwich*, and to *Braintry, Bocking*, and *Colchester*; where 'tis wrought into Stuffs and Bays: A Part of it is used within the County, being Comb'd, and Weav'd into Serges, Tammies and Shaloons, at *Kettering* and other Towns. The Fallow, or shorter Wooll is usually sent into *Yorkshire*, and to the *West*, to *Cirencester*, and *Taunton*, for the making of Cloths.

The trades of woolcombing and worsted-weaving were very late in arriving in Northamptonshire. In 1662 Thomas Fuller wrote, 'Observe we here that mid-England—Northamptonshire, Lincolnshire and Cambridge—having most of the wool have least of the clothing therein'. And by the time John Morton wrote his *Natural History of Northamptonshire* forty or so years later, weaving was only in its infancy. However, it was destined to become an important source of livelihood for the 18th-century poor, whose numbers increased with the overall growth of population at that time.

By no means all enclosure was for permanent pasture, though much of it was. In the period from about 1560 much land was inclosed to enable farmers to practise a new pattern of mixed farming known as 'up-and-down farming', 'ley-farming' or 'convertible-husbandry'. This replaced the permanent arable of the medieval farmers by a rotation of the same land for both cereals and grass. Sometimes this was associated with other improved farming methods such as drainage and the floating of water-meadows. And not all enclosures were carried out by landlords against local wishes. By the 18th century it was often done by local agreement between freeholders registered by a decree in the Chancery or Court of Exchequer. At this time, too, a certain amount of enclosure was of woodland and fen, a process by which the stock of arable land was increased, not diminished. Above all, the extent to which land was enclosed at this time should not be exaggerated. By the time, about 1740 when the Parliamentary Inclosure movement began, it has been estimated that some three-quarters to four-fifths of the parishes of Northamptonshire were still open-field.

Behind the changes caused by enclosure lay pressures of a more fundamental kind which beset peasant societies. In all pre-industrial societies the yield of the annual harvest is all important. In the 17th century, every fourth harvest was, on average, a bad one, and in the Civil War period there were 10 failures in the space of 15 or 16 years. Serious harvest failures led to high bread prices, the danger of famine, and the spread of pestilence. In Northamptonshire there were outbreaks

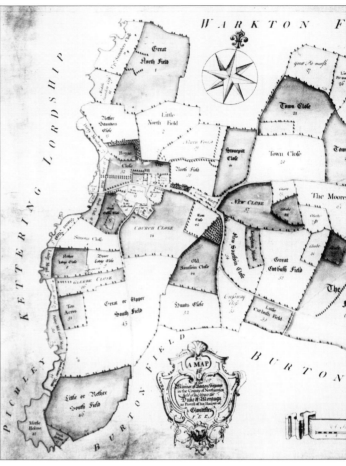

60 *'Ancient inclosure': Brasier's map of Barton Seagrave made for the Duke of Montagu in 1727. Barton was enclosed in 1633 but it is not difficult to identify the former open fields. The names Old Sanfoin Close and New Sanfoin Close indicate the use of one of the new crops of improved husbandry.*

61 *The Montagu Alms-houses, Weekley, for a Master and six brethren. Boldly dated 1611, below the Montagu arms the inscription reads, 'What thou doest do yn Fayth'.*

62 *Charity school, Weekley. The inscription over the door reads, 'A free schoole for Weekley and Werkton fovnded by Nicholas Latham clerke parson of Barnewell St Andrew to teach theire children to write and reade Anno Domini 1624'.*

of the plague in 1578, 1603, 1605, 1638, 1647, and 1665-6, and it was at times when peasant discontent over enclosures coincided with periods of dearth or plague that governments became most alarmed. Yet, despite plague and pestilence in the later Tudor and the Stuart periods, there was a slow overall growth in the population of this country, which was most marked in the case of London. The demand for produce from an increasing population and from an over-large capital had important effects on agriculture over a very wide area. There arose the development of a commercial type of farming which produced for distant rather than local markets. It also brought into being the English regional farming specialisms which, by the end of the 17th century, were well known. Northamptonshire by then had become notable as a grain and wool county.

One of the consequences of these changes, and of another economic feature of the period—the prolonged fall in real wages between 1540 and 1640—was that the English peasantry began to be forced out of existence. This was undoubtedly one of the fears of the Northamptonshire levellers in 1607. A minority of peasants were able to take advantage of new openings for 'commercial' farming and moved up into the ranks of the yeoman, but in time most lost their modest holdings and were reduced to the position of landless labourers. It was not a process which worked itself out very quickly, but by the end of the 18th century the peasant farmer had virtually disappeared in England. In the minds of countrymen the process was inseparable from the spread of enclosure.

One result, in Northamptonshire, as elsewhere in the Midlands, was the distinction which developed between 'open' and 'close' parishes. Open villages, where ownership was fragmented, were ones to which people migrated from parishes where enclosure and depopulation had taken place. This movement was often forced by landlords who owned much or all of a parish, and were able to pull down the former dwellings of the poor and 'close' their villages. Open parishes were usually more populous and came to have a markedly different character. They had more poor, more ne'er-do-wells, more religious diversity, often a range of crafts and (later) small industries. Examples are Long Buckby, Raunds, Brigstock, and King's Cliffe. The close parishes were smaller, had neater houses, were better endowed with charities and schools and, after 1662, were places where chapels were not tolerated to rival the parish church. Although separate, open and close parishes were intimately connected. The former were where the surplus pool of

63 *The former* White Lion Inn, *Oundle. Dated 1641, it was a rebuild of a medieval inn.*

64 The Saracen's Head, *Towcester, one of the best inns on the great road to 'West Chester'.*

labour was housed; and, since under the old Poor Law each parish had to maintain its own poor, the poor of open parishes cost rich farmers in close parishes nothing to maintain, but were near at hand when needed.

Tudor and Stuart Northamptonshire was affected by other economic developments. The growth of population, rural change, and the increasing demands for food and raw materials from a distance led to a resurgence of trade and wayfaring. One result was the revival of the market town after the long later-medieval decline. 'No Village, Parishe, or Place in the Whole Shire is scarcely 4 Myles from some one Markett Towne', wrote John Norden in 1610.[9] And with the late-Tudor and Stuart revival of markets came an increase in the number of fairs in Northamptonshire. Yet, by about 1660, whilst some market towns were flourishing, others, clearly, were not. Wellingborough forged ahead at the expense of Higham Ferrers; Rothwell suffered by being too close to Kettering, and King's Cliffe by its proximity to Stamford. By the time of the Restoration Brackley's importance as a great wool market was a thing of the past, and nobody seriously regarded Great Weldon as a market town any more.

65 *The seals of the boroughs of Higham Ferrers, Northampton, Daventry and Brackley.*

An important factor in the rise and progress of these towns was whether or not they were on a national road. A good example is Towcester, a town which, in Morton's words, 'owes its Improvements to a well frequented Market, and to the Great *West-Chester* Road upon which it stands. One of its Inns has the Best Custom, 'tis generally said, of any single Inn upon the *Chester* Road'. This was the time when the English inn became very important, for much trade into it moved from the market-place. Inns were frequented by a whole new class of wayfaring traders whose business took them up and down the main roads to London—wealthy horse-dealers, wool-staplers, barley-factors and cattle-drovers. Partly because of their favoured situations on these roads, and partly because some had patrons, Northampton, Daventry, Brackley and Higham Ferrers were granted new borough charters by the Crown in the 16th century, giving them close corporations. And Higham Ferrers, Brackley and Peterborough were given the privilege, long enjoyed by Northampton, of sending members to parliament, a distinction which, however, was not extended to Daventry when it was granted a charter in 1576. Yet the subsequent stagnation of Higham and Brackley serves to remind us that a borough charter was not, in itself, enough to ensure economic success.

In the Tudor, Stuart and Georgian era Northamptonshire's towns were centres of exchange rather than manufacture, markets rather than industrial communities, and this remained as true of Northampton as the other, much smaller, towns, despite the fact that its shoemakers could meet very large orders for boots and shoes. Being at once a major local market, a county capital, and situated on a national road, Northampton was the most favourably-placed of all the local towns to rise in economic importance at this time. By 1660 it had about forty inns, and in 1720 this number had increased to about sixty. From the time of Queen Elizabeth to the coming of the railways in the early years of Queen Victoria Northampton thrived, and no other town in the county remotely rivalled it in size or importance.

The Inheritors: The Rise of the County Gentry

'No shire within this land is so plentifullie stored with Gentry, in regard whereof this Shire may seem worthy to be termed the Herald's Garden': so wrote John Norden in 1610.[10] The operative word is 'plentifullie'; by the time of the Civil War it has been estimated that there were as many as 350 families of gentry in Northamptonshire, and the county had become famous for its country houses, which ranged from great Elizabethan 'prodigy houses' down to the modest manor houses of the squires.

The interesting thing is that, with the exception of families such as the Wakes, Vauxes and Knightleys, few of the Caroline gentry of Northamptonshire could trace their lineage back into the Middle Ages. In the Tudor and Stuart period the county underwent a social transformation: it presents a nice example of the phenomenon of the 'rise of the gentry'.

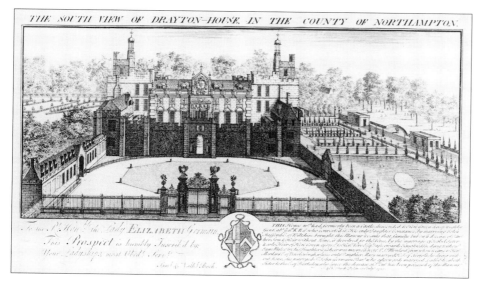

66 *Drayton, near Lowick, in 1729. Essentially a house which retains the form of a castle, it had the hall and range behind the main entrance extensively remodelled by William Talman a few years before this engraving was made by Samuel and Nathaniel Buck. Note the formal gardens in the fashionable style of the time.*

The rise of the Northamptonshire families is partly explained by the familiar story of how old landed families became extinct in the Wars of the Roses, and how the Tudors deliberately promoted a new aristocracy. However, there were other factors at work in Northamptonshire. In the 15th and early 16th centuries the county seems not to have been the power-base of any great family;

67 *The tomb of Sir William Fitzwilliam, 1534, St Mary, Marholm. Henry VIII made him Earl of Southampton and a Knight of the Garter.*

in the reign of Henry VII it had no earl and only one nobleman, Lord Vaux. The new gentry were usually of small landowner origins, and most that rose under the Tudors were native to the county or came from nearby in the Midlands. Again, much of the county in the Middle Ages was forest; it was disafforested on a large scale in the Tudor and Stuart period and it is noticeable that many of the estates of the new gentry were in former forest areas. Before 1540 much of the land was monastic property and came on to the market at just the right time for many of the 'new men' to buy it at favourable prices. Moreover, estates in Northamptonshire were highly desirable; they yielded good rents; no part of the county was above a two-and-a-half day's ride from London; and Northamptonshire had long been famous for its hunting.

Those families which rose to the ranks of the gentry and nobility in this period did so because of their exceptional acquisition of wealth, sometimes rapid, sometimes over several generations, which they used to buy land, build houses, and found dynasties. One avenue to such wealth lay through trade. The fortunes of the Fitzwilliams of Milton, who by the mid-19th century were the most extensive landowners in the county,

68 *The tomb of Sir John Spencer I, who died in 1522, and his wife, in the Spencer chapel, St Mary, Great Brington, described as 'the latest Gothic monument with effigies in the county'.*

were laid by Sir William Fitzwilliam, a merchant tailor who became an alderman of the City of London. He invested his wealth, when, in 1502, he purchased an estate in his native county at Milton and Marholm, near Peterborough. It was rich pastureland and he and his successors increased its value by a zealous policy of inclosure. Another family whose origins were similar is Isham of Lamport. Its founder, John Isham, who made a fortune as a London mercer, was a younger son of a minor gentleman of Pytchley and purchased the Lamport estate in 1560.

Another road to wealth in the later Middle Ages was to specialise in large-scale sheep farming. Two of the most prominent families in Northamptonshire, the Knightleys and the Spencers, owed their rise to the golden fleece. As early as 1416 Richard Knightley purchased the manor of Fawsley, and he and his successors in the next century or so inclosed the parish, depopulated the village, built a manor house, and mounded and ditched a deer-park close by. The Spencers, too, first appear as great sheep farmers in Warwickshire in the second half of the 15th century and built up an estate around Wormleighton in that county. After three generations, in 1508 Sir John Spencer bought the manor of Althorp, near Northampton, which eventually became the country seat of the family.

Other ways to great wealth lay through the law, royal favour, and the service of the state. A great Northamptonshire family was founded by Sir Edward Montagu, Lord Chief Justice under Henry VIII. The son of a minor squire, he returned to his native county in 1528, buying a manor house at Boughton, near Kettering, which had been emparked in the reign of Edward IV. Similarly, the Brudenells were established at

69 *Sir Edward Montagu, robed as Lord Chief Justice.*

Deene in 1514 by Sir Robert Brudenell, Chief Justice of the Court of Common Pleas, and the Griffins at Dingley by Sir Edward Griffin, Attorney-General to Edward VI and Philip and Mary. The Comptons, an old Warwickshire family, later Earls and Marquesses of Northampton, were brought to prominence by the favours Henry VIII bestowed upon Sir William Compton, who grew up with him as a Ward of the Crown. In 1512 Sir William purchased the manors of Ashby David, Yardley Hastings, and six others nearby, which today form the nucleus of one of the greatest county estates. Most rapid of all to rise were those who served, or found favour with, Queen Elizabeth. Two notable Northamptonshire men to do so were Sir Christopher Hatton, her Lord Chancellor, and Sir William Cecil, the first Lord Burghley, Secretary of State and then Lord Treasurer to the Queen. Both were builders of palaces in Northamptonshire, Hatton at Holdenby and Kirby, and Cecil at Burghley.

70 *Sir Christopher Hatton, builder of Holdenby and extender of Kirby Hall.*

71 *The north range of the courtyard of Kirby Hall, the handsomest ruin in England: a loggia with a gallery above and the main gateway into the house. It was built in the 1570s, with additions of 1638-40.*

72 Sir William Cecil, 1st Lord Burghley, Queen Elizabeth's trusted minister and the most powerful man in England in his time.

The availability of land on favourable terms was an important factor in the enlarging and consolidating of the estates of many of these rising Tudor families. For many, the monasteries were dissolved at a fortuitous time, and they were in a position to seize the opportunities presented by a buyers' market. However, other factors should not be overlooked. One sure and certain way to wealth has always been to marry rich women, and the capital which set up John Isham was provided by his marriage to the well-provided-for widow of a fellow London mercer. The wealth of the Comptons was assured when, in 1599, William, Lord Compton, married (against the wishes of her father) the only child of Sir John Spencer, an opulent London merchant, a marriage which eventually brought him not only £300,000 in money, but property in London as well.

In the century from about 1540 the most successful of these families, their financial bases firmly laid, proceeded to enlarge or rebuild their houses and extend their parks. Grandest of all were the 'prodigy houses' of Holdenby, Kirby, Burghley, and Castle Ashby, built to demonstrate

73 John Isham, robed as a rich merchant of the City of London, where he made his fortune.

the status of the family and to entertain and impress Elizabeth or James I. More modest manor houses of the period are to be seen at Fawsley, where Sir Edmund Knightley built a hall with a fine bay window, at Dingley, built by Sir Edward Griffin in the 1550s, and Deene, where a new hall was built by Sir Edmund Brudenell in 1571.

By the early Caroline period the 'new men' were well established and a new aristocracy was rising from their ranks. By the time of the Civil War the Spencers, the Cecils, the Montagus, the Comptons, and the Mordaunts had entered the peerage and the Ishams the baronetcy. Their families had extensively intermarried and there was a pronounced

III *Peterborough Cathedral, with its great west front built in Barnack stone in the Early English style of the early 13th century.*

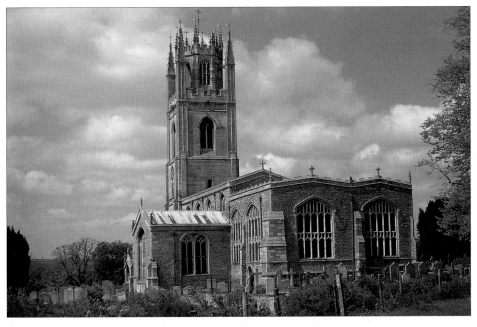

IV *The church of St Peter, Lowick, re-built in the Perpendicular style by the Greene family of Drayton. The tower with its octagonal lantern with eight pinnacles is especially memorable.*

V *Burghley House, one of the greatest, if not the greatest of the 'prodigy houses' of the new Elizabethan aristocracy, in its park. It is still the property of the Cecil family.*

VI *Alabaster monument to Sir Richard Knightley and his wife, 1534, in St Mary's Church, Fawsley.*

sense of 'county community'. One of its sources of strength was the fact that none of the social and economic upheavals of the previous century had led to 'foreigners' moving into the county in any numbers. However, although a few families had graduated to the peerage, the great majority were squires with relatively small estates. In several ways their viewpoint was different from that of the 'grandees'. Some were strong Puritans; a number were active supporters of parliament in its resistance

74 *Altar tomb in St Peter, Deene, with monuments to Sir Robert Brudenell, Chief Justice of the King's Common Bench, and his two wives, 1531.*

to the power of the Crown; and many were feeling the economic strain of the long inflation of the period which made life difficult for those whose income depended solely on rents from modest estates. It was a combination of these influences which made many of the Northamptonshire squires notable resisters to the religious and political policies of Charles I in the 1620s and 1630s.

Catholics and Puritans

At the start of her reign Queen Elizabeth imposed a religious settlement by which she hoped to bridge the gulfs opened up in the previous quarter century. From 1559 the queen was 'Supreme Governor' of the Church of England, and uniformity of worship was to be secured through the Book of Common Prayer and, later, the Thirty-Nine Articles. Nominal conformity was to be enforced, but the queen hoped that coercion would not be needed and that in time all her subjects would come to accept the settlement. For some years it seemed just possible that this might happen. However, from the 1570s Puritan ministers inside the church, and Catholic recusants outside it made this ambition unattainable.

Northamptonshire is not a county where Catholicism survived at all vigorously, and this was undoubtedly because so few of the gentry adhered to the Old Faith. Among those who did the Treshams of Rushton, the Vauxes of Harrowden, the Catesbys of Ashby St Legers, and the Brudenells of Deene were the most prominent. Before 1580 they seemed to have conformed, more or less, to the settlement of 1559. It was the missions of the Jesuit Fathers Parsons and Campion, which started that year, that made them into recusants. For this they paid a high price. In 1581 Sir Thomas Tresham, Lord Vaux and Sir William Catesby were convicted for harbouring priests and fined and imprisoned. From then on the English Catholics were on the horns of a dilemma. They were torn between their patriotism as Englishmen and their natural desire to see the return of England to the Old Faith, the latter being impossible without political intrigue and alliance with their country's enemies.

75 *Detail from the Classical screen at Castle Ashby, c.1630.*

76 *Sir Thomas Tresham (1545 to 1605), the builder of the Triangular Lodge, Rushton and Lyveden New Bield.*

77 *Doorway, Tresham's Triangular Lodge, Rushton*

78 *The Triangular Lodge, Rushton, built in the 1590s.*

No family in England suffered this dilemma more actually than the Treshams of Rushton. From the time of his first imprisonment Sir Thomas Tresham lived the life of a hostage, suffering imprisonment and fines whenever the government felt itself threatened. In all he spent 15 years in prison or under house arrest, despite being known to be 'a very good subject and a great adversary of Spanish practices'.[11] His stubborn adherence to the Old Faith took an eccentric (and enduring) form: he commemorated it in buildings. The first of these was a curious triangular folly at Rushton. It was an involved and elaborate evocation in stone of the mystery of the Holy Trinity (as well as an elaborate pun on his own name and his coat of arms). Less unusual is Lyveden New Bield, his other 'Catholic' building. Planned as a lodge, or summerhouse, to his manor house, near Brigstock, it was designed in the shape of a cross, and (like the triangular lodge) carries inscriptions from the Latin Bible and a repeated pattern of the six symbols of the Passion of Christ.

Tresham and the other Northamptonshire first generation recusant gentlemen studiously avoided involvement in the plots around Mary, Queen of Scots, who, from 1585, was temptingly close—incarcerated in the royal castle at Fotheringhay. There she was tried, and there, in 1587, executed. Yet if Sir Thomas Tresham was loyal to Queen Elizabeth, some of his family were not. His brother was a captain in the service of Spain, and his son Francis was foolish enough to become involved in both Essex's rebellion of 1601 and the Gunpowder Plot four years later. Much influenced by Robert Catesby, the son of another Northamptonshire recusant squire, he was sent to the Tower after the Essex plot, but released after his father paid £2,000 for his pardon. Although only on the fringe of the Gunpowder Plot he was again arrested, and died in the Tower months after succeeding to the estate. The family never recovered: deeply encumbered by debts, the estate was sold in 1614, and the family became extinct upon the death of Sir William Tresham in 1634. Two years before the Treshams, the Catesbys lost their estates and the Brudenells renounced their Catholicism in the early 18th century. Northamptonshire was, and remained into modern times, one of the least Catholic areas in England.

From about 1570 the Elizabethan religious settlement was under attack from another quarter, from inside the ranks of the clergy. A struggle began between the 'Arminians' (or High Churchmen) and the Puritans, whose dream it was to overturn the government of the bishops and rebuild the Church of England on the Presbyterian model of Calvin's Geneva or John Knox's Scotland. The movement was strong in Northamptonshire: it has been said that 'there was no county in England where Puritanism gained such a stronghold, or made such an open demonstration of its objects and methods'. It began in Northampton in 1571 with

79 *Lyveden New Bield, 1604-5.*

80 *Monument to Robert Browne, St Giles' churchyard, Northampton.*

81 *All that remains of the castle at Fotheringhay.*

82 *Wothorpe House.*

83 *Arms of the Isham family.*

the Puritan religious exercises known as 'prophesyings', and for a century the town was a Puritan hotbed. This may well have been because there was an old strain of opposition to religious orthodoxy which went back to the Lollards. It certainly had a lot to do with the connection between the spread of new religious ideas and the growth of trade in this period; the great fairs in London and the provincial towns were ideal settings for the dissemination of ideas from the continent. Puritanism was also encouraged by statesmen such as Sir William Cecil at a time when the throne was only one heartbeat away from being occupied by a Catholic, whose supporters were actively involved in plotting against the queen. And at first the local Puritan clergy were given support by Edmund Scambler, Bishop of Peterborough.

Despite periodic repression, from 1571, when the preacher Percival Wiburn proposed that Northampton should model itself on Calvin's Geneva, the county became a centre of Puritanism. Although Puritan ministers were deprived of their livings (as Wiburn was), they were protected by certain of the gentry, prominent among whom were George Carleton of Overstone and Sir Richard Knightley of Fawsley. Before the end of the queen's long reign there had been three co-ordinated, if thinly supported, attempts to set up a Presbyterian 'shadow' church government, the last being suppressed with great vigour by Archbishop Whitgift (strongly supported by the queen herself). Whitgift's success provoked the famous 'Martin Marprelate' Tracts attacking bishops, produced on a printing press moved on from place to place to avoid detection. For a time it was hidden at Fawsley. In addition to the Presbyterian form of Puritanism, in the later Elizabethan period Northamptonshire became a nursery of 'Independency', or Congregationalism, which was to be the religion of Oliver Cromwell. Until about 1642 this was known as 'Browneism', because the idea that each church should be a single self-governing congregation of the faithful was first expounded by Robert Browne (1550-1632), for more than forty years vicar of Thorpe Achurch, near Oundle.

Although Puritanism among the clergy had been vigorously suppressed by Whitgift, it was not eradicated. But by the end of Elizabeth's reign it had spread widely among the craftsmen and merchants of the towns, and the squires and gentlemen. With the accession of James I, it was hoped that Puritan arguments for reforming the Church of England along Calvinist lines would be given a sympathetic hearing. This was not to be: for presenting a petition from Northamptonshire to parliament against the suspension of Puritan ministers Sir Edward Montagu and Sir Valentine Knightley, the two Knights of the Shire, fell under severe royal displeasure. The consolidation of the Arminians under James I and Charles I was resisted as well as resented in Northamptonshire. Archbishop Laud's visitation of 1633 revealed how 'in no other county in England was there probably the same extreme defiance of rubrics, order and doctrine, as was in the case of some of the parishes in Northamptonshire'.[12] All Saints, Northampton, was singled out for special censure. However, by then Charles I's anti-Puritan regime was approaching its end. When the Long Parliament of 1640 met, the tide turned in favour of the Puritans.

The Civil War and Commonwealth

Puritanism was not the only source of opposition to the government of Charles I, though the Puritans were at the centre of everything. The squires were incensed by the king's attempts to rule without parliament, especially during the 'Eleven Years' Tyranny' (1629-40). In those years there was much resistance in Northamptonshire to the taxes of the king's government. Individual gentlemen were fined for refusing to pay 'forced loans' and not taking up their knighthoods. Fines, amounting to £80,000 in total, were levied on certain landowners for transgressing ancient forest laws, specially revived in 1635-9. And among the lesser gentry there was a spirit of resistance to Ship Money which grew with each levy. In 1638 the Sheriff complained 'few or none will pay without distress; others wilfully oppose his servants in making distresses; and lastly, others by no fair persuasion yield assistance for assessing themselves and others, their tenants within their parishes'.[13] The sum-total of grievances against the king was expressed in a Petition to the recalled parliament in April 1640 from the freeholders of Northamptonshire. It

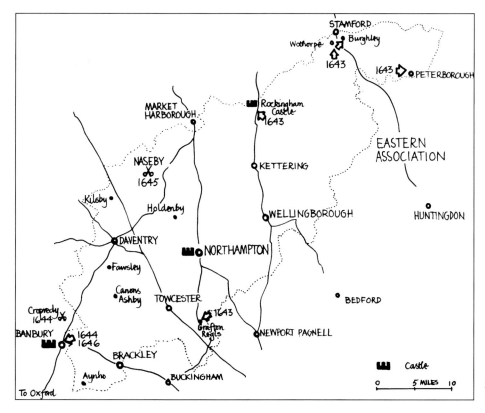

84 *The Civil War in Northamptonshire.*

85 *Spencer Compton, Earl of Northampton, killed in 1643 fighting for the king.*

stated 'of late we have been unusually and unsupportably charged, troubled and grieved in our consciences, persons, and estates by innovation in religion, exactions in spiritual courts, molestations of our most Godly and learned ministers, ship money, monopolies, undue impositions, army money, waggon money, house money, conduct money, and enlarging the forest beyond the ancient bounds, and the like; for not yielding to such things or some of them, divers of us have been molested, distrained and imprisoned'.[14]

When the king's personal government collapsed in 1640 in the face of the Scottish Covenanters the county returned strongly Puritan M.P.s to both the Short and Long Parliaments. The enemies of Charles I were in no mood to be forgiving: they insisted on the redress of grievances, the removal, trial and execution of Strafford and Laud, and the granting of the claims of parliament. The king was clearly defeated, though he failed to comprehend it. However, events in the next two years, in which the Presbyterian attacks on the Church of England alienated many in parliament, led to the growth of new

86 *Henry Spencer, 1st Earl of Sunderland, also killed in 1643 fighting for the king.*

support for the king. After his failure to arrest the five members in early 1642, he left London and events moved inexorably towards war.

It came as no surprise that Northampton declared for parliament in 1642. Vehemently Puritan, it had opposed the king over Ship Money, refused him a contribution towards the army to fight the Scots, armed its citizens and repaired its walls. In the war it had the strongest garrison in the South Midlands. Northampton's support for parliament was based on a combination of holiness and hard-headedness; from 1642 the orders placed in the town for boots for the army, and the ability of the local dealers to meet the extensive demands for horses, did much to increase the wealth of some of the town.

The county was virtually surrendered to parliament by the royalist gentry, who left their estates to join the king. Their leader was the 2nd Earl of Northampton, who fought at Worcester, Banbury and Stafford, and was killed at Hopton Heath in 1643. The 3rd Baron Spencer took £10,000 to the king, and was created Earl of Sunderland, but was also killed in 1643, at Newbury. Also prominent among the king's supporters were the Wakes, the Ishams and Catholics such as the Vauxes and the Brudenells. Many of the lesser gentry, however, were strongly parliamentarian, and such families as the Cartwrights, Claypoles, Drydens, Knightleys, and Thorntons were the backbone of the County Committee. Some moved into Northampton both for security and also to reinforce the rule of the Godly, and the town was resolutely controlled by borough corporation and County Committee all through the war. In Colonel Whetham, by origin a London baker, it had an able military governor.

In 1642 the parliamentarians in Northamptonshire were quickly in action. When Lord Montagu put into execution the royal commission of array he was arrested and sent to the Tower of London, and at Brackley they cut off supplies and money being delivered to the king by Sir John Biron. The first significant blows in the Midlands, however, were struck by the king—in October he defeated parliament at Edgehill in Warwickshire, afterwards making Oxford his headquarters. Banbury was taken and, under the command of Sir William Compton, brother of the 2nd Earl of Northampton, was the main outpost of royalist Oxford in this district until its fall in 1646.

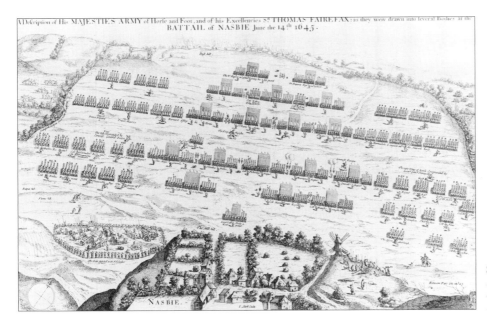

87 *Engraving of the line-up of the two armies before the battle of Naseby, 14 June 1645.*

88 *The site of the battle of Naseby and the modern memorial to it.*

In 1643 the war in the county assumed the form it was going to take for the duration: parliament, through its garrisons at Northampton and Newport Pagnell, defending the flanks of the Puritan Eastern Counties and keeping the main roads from London open to the passage of men and supplies, and both sides raiding into the disputed territory between Banbury and Watling Street. At the start the parliamentary forces mopped up the few royalist strong points in the county. This first became necessary when royalists from Belvoir Castle and Newark captured Stamford. Colonel Cromwell was despatched with guns and cavalry to drive them out: the defenders retreated to Wothorpe House and then Burghley, which was stormed. Later, Cromwell's troops wantonly desecrated Peterborough Cathedral. In the same year parliamentary forces seized Rockingham Castle and took Grafton House. The royalist forces made several sallies into the county in that year. In May they won a skirmish in the 'town field' at Middleton Cheney, and in October a raiding party from Banbury made for Northampton via Daventry, Long Buckby, Holdenby and Chapel Brampton. After a skirmish at the north gate of the town they veered away to Olney, seizing horses from friend and foe alike along the route. They then moved on to Towcester, the object being to cut the road to London. The following January they withdrew to attack Aylesbury. In the winter of 1643-44 parliament made the attempt to form regional associations to overcome the weakness resulting from each county raising troops for its own defences alone. This was not very effective: the Midland Association, in which Northamptonshire, Buckinghamshire and Leicestershire were combined, was rent by dissention. Only the counties in the Eastern Association were united. In 1644 the foraging policy of both sides in West Northamptonshire carried on, and until the battle of Marston Moor in July, when they suffered a major defeat in the north, the initiative generally lay with the king's forces. By August it was the turn of the local parliamentarian forces to go on the offensive, the objective being the capture of Banbury Castle. In this they failed, and withdrew as winter came on.

In the winter of 1644-45 the New Model Army replaced the Associations. Deliberately created to counter the problem of narrow county allegiance, it proved to be the most effective fighting force yet raised in England. In early 1645, however, both the local royalist forces and the king's main army were on the offensive in the Midlands. In May the king took Leicester and sacked it, and then withdrew towards Oxford. Events were moving towards a major confrontation: both sides began

89 *Holdenby House in the 18th century. A few years after the sojourn there of Charles I, it was bought by a parliamentarian asset-stripper and largely demolished.*

concentrating their main forces in the Midlands. The king ordered Goring to bring his forces from the West Country to join him, and his failure to do so spelt ruin. Meanwhile, Fairfax, as Commander-in-Chief of the New Model Army, was mustering his forces in the district after taking Oxford. In early June the king, hearing the enemy was near, retreated to Market Harborough, followed by the New Model Army. On the 14th the royalists moved up to Naseby to fight. It was the deciding battle of the Civil War. After seizing the initiative against a numerically stronger foe, the king was finally defeated by the military skill of Cromwell and his cavalry. The king surrendered to the Scots shortly after, and in return for 'back pay' of £400,000 they handed him over to parliament. In February 1646 he was put under house-arrest in Holdenby House near Northampton, and stayed there until seized from the hands of parliament by the army the following year. After the battle of Naseby the war did not last much longer locally; Banbury fell after a siege in 1646, and royalist resistance in the area collapsed.

The county experienced its full share of the turbulence and upheavals which followed the end of the fighting, the quarrels between parliament and the army, and the events which led to the execution of Charles I in 1649. In that fateful year starving men in Wellingborough, inspired by Digger ideas, began to cultivate the town common, issuing a 'Declaration' setting out their reasons. In that year, too, William Thompson, a Leveller captain, rode into Northampton, bluffed the authorities, seized weapons and recruited a few to his cause. He was, however, overtaken at Walgrave and killed by soldiers fresh from suppressing the Leveller mutiny at Burford.

Under the Commonwealth two groups suffered particularly—the clergy and the royalist gentry. From 1643 a Presbyterian regime was nominally established in the Church of England, though the army forced it to tolerate Baptists and Independents: Quakers, Unitarians,

Episcopalians and Catholics were not so lucky. The bishop of Peterborough was deprived of his office and income, and in some 96 parishes in Northamptonshire the clergy were ejected and replaced by Presbyterian 'intruders'. Any minister using the Book of Common Prayer in church faced the risk of banishment from the realm. The lands of royalist gentry were seized by the Committee for the Sequestration of the Estates of Delinquents, and before they could enjoy their rents again they had to negotiate an appropriate fine with the Committee for Compounding: before he could re-possess his estates, the Earl of Northampton had to pay £14,000. Catholic gentlemen faced extra fines for popish recusancy, and there was a Committee for the Sale of Delinquents Estates.

In the years after the end of the first Civil War in 1646 many of the former opponents of the king among the gentry were alienated by the consequences of the victory of Cromwell and the New Model. For some the refusal of the army to disband in 1646 was the signal to withdraw; for others it was the failure of the plan with the Scots to set up a Presbyterian church and throne; for most it was the execution of the king in 1649 after the Second Civil War. They viewed with dismay the way the control of affairs under the Commonwealth often passed to men of the 'middling sort' and soldiers such as Major William Butler of Oundle. From the ranks of such men were drawn the members of the powerful Commissioners for Militia to Suppress Insurrections and Preserve the Peace for the Counties of Northampton and Rutland after the royalist rising in 1648. And even more the gentry resented the centralised direction of events under Cromwell, one of the things most disliked during the Eleven Years' Tyranny.

However, the situation was not as revolutionary as it seemed. Cromwell could not work with parliament, and he found, as Charles I had found before him, he could not rule without it, at least not for very long. And he was not immortal. As time passed it became clear that those unhappy under the Commonwealth had but to sit tight and wait. Within two years of the Lord Protector's death the monarchy had been restored. Above all the Restoration was a victory for the gentry; not just for those who had fought for Charles I, but for those who opposed him. The career of Sir Richard Knightley illustrates this. Presbyterian by family tradition and closely associated with the opponents of Charles I in parliament (he was married to Hampden's daughter) he sat in the Short Parliament and the Long. He signed the Solemn League and Covenant, but refused to aid the plans for trying the king, for which he spent a short time as a prisoner of the army. He might have been Speaker of Richard Cromwell's parliament; but by then he saw the tide was turning. He sat as one of the Council of State which recalled Charles II, and at the Coronation the Puritan statesman became a Knight of the Bath. After 1662, along with virtually all the erstwhile Puritan gentry, the Knightleys dropped Presbyterianism and accepted the restored Church of England. Thereafter they were pillars of King-and-Church Toryism, and the family tradition of producing men who sat in parliament as Knights of the Shire continued almost uninterrupted to the late 19th century.

4

Restoration and Georgian Northamptonshire

The Heyday of the Great Landowners

The principal beneficiaries of the Restoration and the Glorious Revolution of 1688 were the landed gentry, and their dominance of English life lasted beyond the Reform Act of 1832. In socially conservative Northamptonshire, to which the forces of industrialisation came slowly and late, their leadership was scarcely challenged until the 1880s.

Land brought them not only very considerable wealth from rents, but the prestige of local leadership. It also made them literally Lords of Creation; the rural landscape was made and re-made through their inclosures, parks and landscape-gardening, processes which, as we have seen, involved the transplanting of people as well as trees. Local leadership was recognised by elevation to the magistracy, and as Justices of the Peace they not only presided over law and order in the countryside, but also the government of the county through the Court of Quarter Sessions. They were as much a political as an economic class; their estates constituted effective local spheres of political influence, and electors in both county and boroughs were expected to vote 'so as not to disoblige their landlord'. And Northamptonshire was pre-eminently a county of landed estates. In the 'Return of the Owners of Land' in 1873, the so-called 'New Domesday Book', 57 per cent of the land was owned by 102 landlords with estates of a thousand acres or more, and just under half of this was in the hands of 16 persons owning estates of between 5,000 and 20,000 acres.

The nature of landed society in Northamptonshire, though stable, was by no means unchanging. In the hundred or so years from about 1640 the relative position of the different discernible groups within the landed classes underwent drastic changes. The 'parish gentry', the relatively small landowners who were so numerous and so active in local life in 1640, were a vanishing breed a century later. The aristocrats, on the other hand, had grown in numbers, and the proportion of the land they held in the county was greater in 1740 than a century earlier. It was they, very largely, who had bought up the estates of the parish gentry. Of the three broad categories of landed gentlemen it was the substantial squires, whose ranks included such families as the Ishams, Cartwrights, Wakes and Drydens, who remained the most stable and unchanging

90 *Easton Neston House (detail).*

75

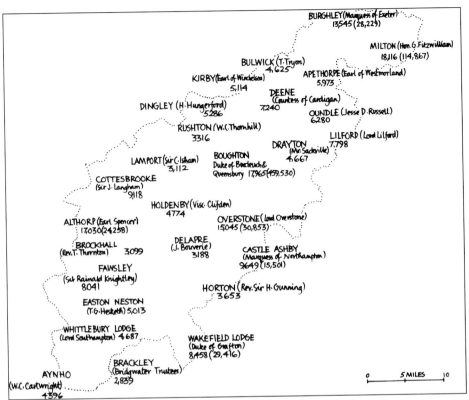

BURGHLEY (Marquess of Exeter)
13,545 (28,229)

MILTON (Hon. G. Fitzwilliam)
18,116 (114,867)

BULWICK (T. Tryon)
4,625

APETHORPE (Earl of Westmorland)
5,973

KIRBY (Earl of Winchilsea)
5,114

DEENE (Countess of Cardigan)
7,240

DINGLEY (H. Hungerford)
5,286

OUNDLE (Jesse D. Russell)
6,280

RUSHTON (W. C. Thornhill)
3,316

LILFORD (Lord Lilford)
7,798

DRAYTON (Mr. Sackville)
4,667

LAMPORT (Sir C. Isham)
3,112

BOUGHTON
Duke of Buccleuch &
Queensbury 17,965 (459,530)

COTTESBROOKE
(Sir J. Langham)
9,118

HOLDENBY (Visc. Clifden)
4,774

OVERSTONE (Lord Overstone)
15,045 (30,853)

ALTHORP (Earl Spencer)
17,030 (24,258)

DELAPRE
(J. Bouverie)
3,188

CASTLE ASHBY
(Marquess of Northampton)
9,649 (15,501)

BROCKHALL
(Rev. T. Thornton) 3,099

FAWSLEY
(Sir Rainald Knightley)
8,041

HORTON (Rev. Sir H. Gunning)
3,653

EASTON NESTON
(T. G. Hesketh) 5,013

WHITTLEBURY LODGE
(Lord Southampton) 4,687

WAKEFIELD LODGE
(Duke of Grafton)
8,458 (29,416)

BRACKLEY
(Bridgwater Trustees)
2,839

AYNHO
(W. C. Cartwright)
4,396

0   5 MILES   10

91   The estates of the 'great landowners of Northamptonshire', based on the Return of Owners of Land of 1873. Only 'great estates' of 3,000 acres and over are shown, which is why the Wake estate at Courteenhall is omitted. The figures given indicate the acreage owned in Northamptonshire: those in brackets indicate the total acreage owned in Great Britain and Ireland, exclusive of urban land holdings.

92   Aristocrat as soldier: the most famous Brudenell of them all, the Earl of Cardigan who led the charge of the Light Brigade in the Crimean War—and survived.

element in landed society. The most successful had by then adopted life-styles within their means, and some of them have survived to the present. Overall, in the 250 years after the Civil War there was a considerable reduction in the number of ancient county families in Northamptonshire. The 350 families of the time of Charles I had, by 1906, been reduced to twenty or so, though these had been joined by rich newcomers.

In the late 17th century something of a gulf opened up between the squires and the aristocrats. It was partly about differences in wealth, and partly about the control of the local areas of political influence. Great county families such as the Fitzwilliams, Spencers and the Montagus were also land-owners in other parts of the country as well as Northamptonshire. These Whig grandees were often men prominent nationally—as peers of the realm, politicians, admirals, soldiers or ambassadors. The squires, however, were more narrowly identified with Northamptonshire; politically they were mostly Tory, and their sphere was the House of Commons. They idealised themselves as the independent guardians of English liberties and regarded the two county parliamentary seats as theirs. Between 1700 and 1806 Northamptonshire invariably returned two Tory Knights of the Shire to Westminster, and they usually included an Isham, a Knightley, or a Cartwright. In the 18th century 'the peace of the county' was rarely disturbed by expensive contested elections. When, in 1806, Viscount Althorp, Earl Spencer's heir and a leading Whig, intervened and caused a contest, indignation among the squires ran high. However, from then until the election of 1831, they had to be satisfied with one Tory and Lord Althorp as the Members for Northamptonshire. Their feelings can be imagined when, at the 1831 election, on the full tide of Reform, *two* Whigs were elected. The squires always maintained that the preserve of the Whig party should be the Northamptonshire boroughs. Higham Ferrers and Peterborough were in the pocket of Earl Fitzwilliam; Brackley was a rotten borough in the gift of the Duke of Bridgewater; and Northampton was by tradition the joint preserve of the Earl of Northampton and the Earl of Halifax. The squires derived no small satisfaction when, in 1768, Earl Spencer intervened in the Northampton election, and there ensued 'the most violent contest for aristocratic pre-eminence' for years.[15] It was reputed to have cost the three earls £160,000, and Lords Northampton and Halifax were ruined by it.

93 *Teapot commemorating the famous 'Three Earls' election of 1768, now in Northampton Art Gallery and Museum.*

The divisions within landed society in this period should not be exaggerated: they were merely the rivalries of an increasingly narrow caucus of families who dominated the shire, whose differences were less than their shared similarity in outlook. One interest which united squire and grandee alike was the thrill of the chase. Northamptonshire had long been one of the chief centres of hunting in England. By the mid-18th century the sport of fox-hunting was beginning to be formalised, a process connected with the re-landscaping of the Midland countryside by the Parliamentary Inclosure movement. The chase was made more exciting by the obstacles presented to the rider by the fences and hedges of the new enclosures, and thickets and fox coverts were deliberately

94 *Fireplace at Lamport by John Webb, 1655.*

95 *A detail of the engraving of a painting by W. and H. Barraud of the meet of the Pytchley Hounds at Crick, about 1851.*

planted when the open-fields were enclosed. Another shared passion was for architecture and formal and landscape-gardening. In the century following the Restoration dozens of country houses in Northampton-shire were remodelled or built anew. Although the grandest architectural conceptions of this period were those of the aristocracy, many of the squires built houses which remain notable in the architectural heritage of Northamptonshire. One such is Lamport. Even before the end of the Commonwealth the royalist baronet Sir Justinian Isham added a new block to his manor house, in the Italian Classical style, using the talents of John Webb, the son-in-law of Inigo Jones. Very few houses, however, were fully rebuilt at any one time, and in the case of Lamport the wings added to Webb's palazzo, forming the modern south west front, were not constructed until the 1730s. The rest of the house was rebuilt in the 1820s, the 1840s and the 1860s. A generation later Sir William Fermor made plans for a new house at Easton Neston, and, wanting one in the contemporary baroque style, sought the services of Sir Christopher Wren. In the event, the rebuilding of Easton Neston fell to Wren's protégé, Nicholas Hawksmoor, who, when Fermor married a rich heiress and became Baron Lempster, was happy to oblige with an appropriately grander scheme, clothing the original brick in Helmdon stone.

At the same time as Hawksmoor was at work on a house which (to some) invites comparison with the Petit Trianon at Versailles, there was a project afoot to build an imitation of the palace of Versailles itself in Northamptonshire. This was at Boughton, near Kettering, where, in the 1690s, Ralph, later the 1st Duke of Montagu, a former ambassador to the court of Louis XIV, and a devotee of French architecture, rebuilt his ancestral home on a prodigious scale. Although not as immense as Versailles, with its seven courtyards, 12 entrances, 52 chimney stacks, and

365 windows, Boughton is the largest country house in the county. To set it off the Duke also laid out in the manner of Le Notre 'the greatest formal French garden in England'. The 2nd Duke of Montagu also liked to do things on a massive scale, but his passion was landscape-gardening rather than building. The 70 miles of avenues of elms and limes he planted on his estates around Boughton, many of which still survive, explain his nickname of 'John the Planter', and there are fewer better examples of the aristocracy acting as Lords of Creation than he and his father. The irony is that, not long after all this replanning, which cost a fortune, Boughton fell into neglect. The male line of the Montagus of Boughton came to an end in 1753 and the

96 *The 1st Duke of Montagu (1638 to 1709).*

estates passed by marriage to the Dukes of Buccleuch and Queensberry. With estates of over half a million acres in England and Scotland, the Buccleuchs were the second largest landowners in Britain, and, possessing 10 great houses, it is scarcely surprising that they rarely visited Boughton, whose formal gardens fell into neglect.

Dukes' houses are one thing, earls' are another. Althorp, the country seat of the Spencers, was remodelled in an altogether more piecemeal

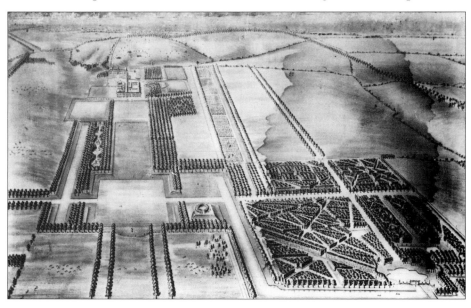

97 *Versailles in Northamptonshire. Rather stained panoramic engraving of the formal gardens at Boughton House, near Kettering, showing the canals, water features, formal gardens, walks, mounts and plantations.*

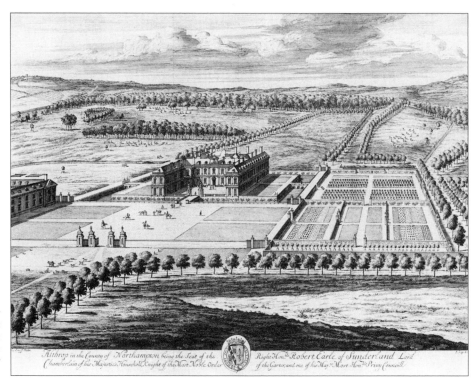

98 *Althorp House, as it was in the late 17th century. John Evelyn called it 'a palace with staterooms as may become a great prince'.*

99 *Plaque and view of Pytchley Hunt Kennels, Brixworth.*

way. The old house itself was enlarged between 1660 and 1680. Then, before 1733, the 3rd Earl of Sunderland, the grandson (and successor) of the Duke of Marlborough, built the fine Palladian stables and had the interior of the house redesigned. The new entrance hall with its local hunting scenes has been called 'the noblest Georgian room in the county'. It was not until the later part of the 18th century, however, that the house took on its present appearance when Henry Holland refaced it with the grey brick, 'mathematical tiles' and stone dressings familiar to the modern visitor to Althorp.

By 1790, when Henry Holland was at work at Althorp, the great period of house-building in the county was largely over. Northamptonshire is relatively rich in houses from the Elizabethan to the late Georgian, but is decidedly thin in Regency and Victorian examples. This perhaps reflects what was happening socially. By 1800 landed society in the county had been secure and stable for a long time, and its heyday was by no means over; it was to last to the send of Queen Victoria's reign. However, stability had brought a rigidity and a conservatism which was as much mental as political. The country gentlemen who extended or altered their houses in the 19th century were usually content to do so in styles consonant with what was there already, and rich newcomers settled for the instant prestige a venerable house brought them. Only one Victorian was confident enough to rebuild in the modern manner—Samuel Jones Loyd, Baron Overstone.

VII *Part of the map of Northampton made by Marcus Pierce in 1632. It has one of only two impressions of what medieval All Saints church looked like (bottom, centre), and also gives a view of the site of the Abbey of St Andrew's about a century after its dissolution (centre left margin).*

VIII *The Mayor's seat in All Saints, Northampton, dating from the mayoralty of Richard White in 1680. It gives a visual impression of the firm connection between the Church, the State and the bodies which governed incorporated towns from the Restoration to the early years of the reign of Queen Victoria.*

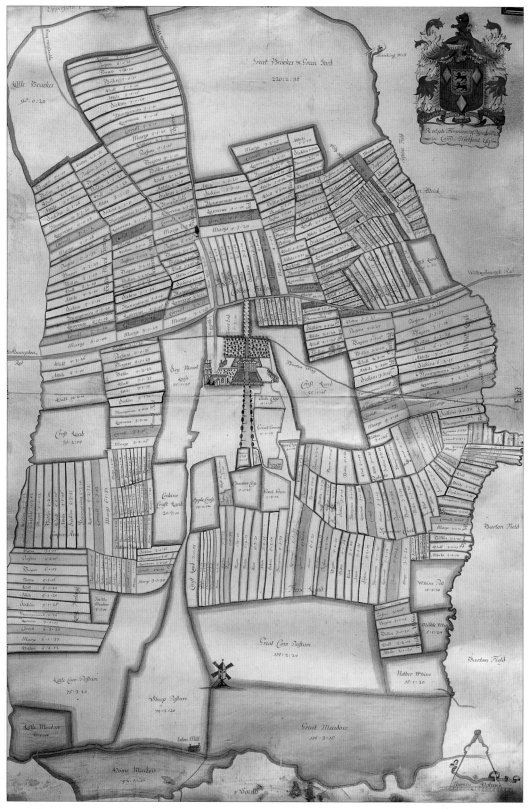

IX *A fine estate map of 1703 of Ecton, near Northampton, a parish in the Nene Valley.*

About 1860 he rebuilt Overstone Hall, the country house bought near Northampton by his banker-father, with a fine disregard for tradition perhaps appropriate to one described as 'the wealthiest, perhaps, of Her Majesty's subjects'.[16]

100 *Overstone Hall. It belonged to Lord Overstone, the opulent banker, and then to Lord and Lady Wantage (Lady Wantage being Lord Overstone's only child). It is now a school.*

Stuart and Georgian Northampton

The decline of Northampton's population and trade in the later Middle Ages was very prolonged. As far as can be judged from the rather imprecise statistics we have, it was not until the second half of the reign of Queen Elizabeth that its population recovered to that at the peak of the medieval expansion in the early 14th century. And in the first half of the 17th century the growth of population was checked by four visitations of the plague—in 1603, 1605, 1638 and 1647. The outbreak in 1638 was extremely severe, with as many as 665 deaths in the town compared with an annual average at that time of 122. However, with the slow growth of population and the national revival of inland trade, in the last 20 years of the 16th century Northampton's fortunes began to improve. The borough charters of 1495 and 1566 make mention of only two fairs; the charter of 1599 mentions seven. In the next 200 years Northampton became a thriving market town and county capital.

Its wealth in this period was created by its weekly markets and annual fairs, and its servicing of wayfaring traders on the great road to Leicester, Manchester and the North-West. Within the town were a remarkable range of crafts and trades, certain of which depended

BRASS IN S.T SEPULCHRE'S CHURCH, NORTHAMPTON.

101 *Brass in St Sepulchre, Northampton, of George Coles and his two wives, about 1640. They are all modishly dressed, as one would expect of an opulent draper. The date is a late one for a commemorative brass.*

on the patronage of the country gentry, many of whom, in the 17th and early 18th centuries, moved into Northampton in winter. At this time the town's economy rested not on industries producing goods for wholesale distribution, but on crafts and commerce. This period was the golden age of English craftsmanship; in the time of Queen Elizabeth some 45 distinct crafts and trades were carried on in the town, and by the time of the first of the Georges these had grown to one hundred and fourteen. By far the greatest were those using leather; it had been so in the Middle Ages, and they grew ever more important after cloth-making faded away in the reign of Henry VIII.

The shoe-trade grew out of an ancient tanning industry which originated with the plentiful supply of animal skins from the Northampton butchers and oak-bark from the woodlands of the county; annual sales of Northamptonshire oak-bark for tanning continued well into the second half of the 19th century. The wars of the 17th century, however, gave the Northampton shoe trade a great boost. In 1642 a large order for shoes for the army setting forth for Ireland was placed in the town, and there were further orders in 1651 and 1688-9, by which year Northampton was also exporting footwear to the plantations. John Morton in 1712 mentions this export trade as well as the supplying of Marlborough's army in Flanders. In the 17th century there seems to have been a flourishing hosiery trade as well, for in 1662 Thomas Fuller declared 'the town of Northampton may be said to stand chiefly on other men's legs; where (if not the best) the most and cheapest boots and stockings are bought in England'.[17] The trade of large-scale shoemaking, however, long remained a Northampton rather than a Northamptonshire speciality; it was not until the last quarter of the 18th century that the trade began to spread to towns such as Wellingborough and Kettering.

Besides shoemakers, tanners, harness and saddle-makers and other tradesmen working leather, there was a range of other crafts, including those which produced goods and services for the fine living of the country gentry—plasterers and stucco artists, cabinet makers, clock-makers, coach builders, writing masters, dancing masters, professors of music and peruke makers. Examples of some of their work can still be seen in houses such as Lamport Hall, where the fine plasterwork was executed by John Woolston, one of a family of 18th-century Northampton plasterers.

Much of the town's wealth was earned by its weekly markets and annual fairs. 'It has several Fairs, and a New Market that is celebrated for

the Best Horses of *England.* The ordinary Markets are stored with Plenty
of all kinds of Rural, and Marketable
Commodities' noted Morton, and
Daniel Defoe in 1720 observed that
there were no less than four horse-
fairs a year. 'Here they buy horses of
all sorts, as well for the saddle as for
the coach and cart.' For travellers
through the town there were 60 inns
by the early 18th century, of which
the three principal were the *George,*
the *Peacock* and the *Red Lion.* Defoe
declared 'the great inn at the George
... looks more like a palace than an
inn and cost about £2,000 building'.[18]

The need to rebuild the *George*
in the late 17th century arose out of
the greatest misfortune to befall the
town since the time of the Norman
Conquest—the Great Fire of 1675.
This started in a house near the site
of the castle, sweeping across the town

THE
State of Northampton
From the beginning of the
FIRE,
Sept. 20th 1675. to Nov. 5th.
Reprefented in a *Letter* to a FRIEND
in LONDON; And now recommen-
ded to all well difpofed Perfons, in
order to Chriftian-Charity, and fpee-
dy Relief for the faid diftreffed
Town and People.

By a Country Minifter.

Licenfed, *Nov.* 22. 1675. *Roger L'eftrange.*

LONDON,
Printed for *Jonathan Robinfon,* at the *Golden Lion* in St.
Pauls Churchyard, and *William Cockeraine* Book-
feller in NORTHAMPTON. 1675.

102 *Title page,* The
State of Northampton
from the Beginning of
the Fire ..., *1675.*

blown by a strong west wind. More than 600 houses and many of the
principal buildings, including All Saints church, were destroyed. The general
loss of property was put at about £150,000, the town shopkeepers having
recently restocked at Stourbridge Fair. A special Act of Parliament was
secured to empower a body of Commissioners to supervise the rebuilding,
and its enactment was speeded by the Recorder of the borough, the 6th
Earl of Northampton. In response to 'parish briefs' and special sermons
preached all over England, aid to the tune of £25,000 arrived in Northampton to help rebuild the town. King Charles II himself gave 1,000 tons
of timber and a remission of taxes towards the rebuilding of All Saints
church.

Although the fire gave Northampton the opportunity to replan the
town anew, by and large it was rebuilt on the same lines as before. The
main street-improvements were brought about by shortening the new All
Saints and opening up the street at the bottom of the Drapery, and widening the entrances to the Market Place. However, the town was graced
by some fine new buildings. In 1658 one traveller described Northampton
as 'an old town, but indifferently handsome, notwithstanding the plenty of
stone dug in that county'. After the rebuilding Defoe found it the 'handsomest and best built town in all this part of England ... The great new
church, the town hall, the jayl, and all their public buildings are the finest
in any country town in England being all built new'. It was once thought
that the new All Saints, 'the finest expression in ecclesiastical terms of the
Age of Wren outside London',[19] was the work of the great architect of

103 *The Great Mace,*
c.*1661.*

104 *All Saints, North-ampton, rebuilt after the Fire to the design of Henry Bell of King's Lynn. The portico, said to be a copy of that of Old St Paul's, was added in 1701.*

105 *The Sessions House, George Row, Northampton, another of Henry Bell's works, in 1747, when it was the County Hall.*

THE COUNTY HALL.
The Cupola being out of repair has been taken down.

106 *Statue of Charles II on the portico of All Saints, Northampton, garlanded with oak. Although the commem-oration of Oak Apple Day as a national holiday ended in 1859, the vicar and churchwardens of the church carried on and to this day commemorate 29 May.*

St Paul's himself, or was perhaps built to one of his designs. However, no evidence has been found to connect Wren with Northampton, and it is now known that this church, to-gether with the Sessions House (Defoe's 'town hall') and the *Peacock* inn, were the work of a less famous but still talented gentleman-architect, Henry Bell, alderman and twice mayor of King's Lynn. The surviving buildings of Northampton after the fire are to this day the focal points of the town centre: it is well-nigh impossible for a Northamp-tonian to imagine the town without the portico, Gothic tower, and dome and lantern of All Saints. Yet the rebuilt church is not merely an ar-chitectural reminder of this period; All Saints is a lesson in stone on the political history of Northampton in the last third of the 17th century.

In the Civil War Northampton was resolutely for the parliament against the king. When the monar-chy was restored the town was pun-ished for its former allegiance. In 1662 the castle and town walls were de-molished, and the corporation thor-oughly purged. The town had to pay £200 for the renewal of its charter and henceforward all members of the corporation had to be members of the Church of England, and the appoint-ment of any new Recorder or Town Clerk had to be confirmed by the Crown. From being Puritan and par-liamentarian the corporation now became Anglican and Tory, and remained so until the Municipal Cor-porations Act of 1835. In the Great Fire 'the cathedral of Northampton-shire puritanism' was burned to the ground: the new All Saints which arose, with a statue of Charles II on its portico and a magnificent pew for

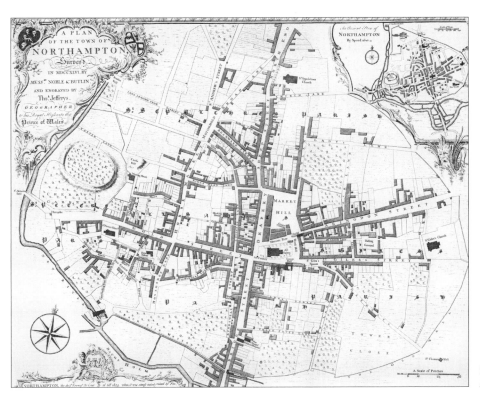

107 *Jefferys' map of Northampton, 1747.*

the mayor in the nave, stands as a reminder of the alliance of Crown, Tory close corporation and Church which dominated the town politically from 1662 to the age of Reform.

There was to come a time when this domination was to be overthrown. In the 18th century Northampton had a sizeable minority of Dissenters who grew more numerous and confident as time wore on. When the shoe trade began to expand, most of the new manufacturers were Dissenters in religion and Whig in politics, and began to demand their share of political power. However, in 1790 these developments were still round the corner; Northampton was still, socially as well as politically, following the same pattern it had since 1662. Although its population had started to grow it was still only about 7,000 souls, and the town was still physically contained within the old medieval limits. In the *Universal Directory* of 1791 no wholesale shoe-manufacturers are listed, though there was one worsted manufacturer and two owners of a cotton mill (which was not destined to survive). As late as this Northampton was still a small pre-Industrial town.

Churchmen and Dissenters

The return of the monarchy in 1660 led to a new attempt to impose religious uniformity through the restoration of the Church of England to

108 *Law's Library, Kings Cliffe. Over the door is the inscription, 'Books of piety are here lent to any persons of this and ye Neighbouring Towns'. The collection is now in the County Record Office.*

its old position of supremacy. The Church's supporters in parliament were in no mood to be either forgiving or tolerant, and proceeded to pass a series of Acts, the objects of which were to force the clergy to conform to the new settlement and to penalise those who refused so that they and their supporters would be forced out of existence in the course of time. The most important of these statutes was the Act of Uniformity of 1662. It required all clergymen, schoolmasters and university fellows to accept on oath the Book of Common Prayer as the only legal service book, and gave them until St Bartholomew's Day (24 August) that year to do so. As elsewhere, the great majority in Northamptonshire took the oath: the 46 who refused were ejected from their livings, and became the original 'Dissenters'.

Under this legislation the once-strong support for Puritanism in Northamptonshire faded after 1662. Significantly, the country gentlemen who had once been its leaders showed no inclination to follow it into the wilderness of Dissent; families such as the Knightleys and the Maunsells cast off their Presbyterianism and thereafter became firm adherents of the Church of England and Toryism. Only time would tell whether or not the Puritan remnant would wither away, but churchmen were determined to ensure it would never again be a power in the land. The laws of the so-called 'Clarendon Code' barred Dissenters from meeting and preaching, sitting on borough corporations, entering parliament, becoming officers in the armed forces, educating their sons at the universities, and joining the learned professions.

The disabilities of the Dissenters received no sympathy from churchmen. In 1660, some twelve years after the death of his ejected predecessor, a bishop returned to Peterborough, and he and his clergy settled into their inheritance and consigned such problems to the waste-bin of history. Ironically, they, too, were soon faced with not dissimilar issues of conscience. In 1695 Bishop White of Peterborough became one of the first 'non-jurors' when he refused to take the oath accepting William and Mary, and was deprived of his living. Thereafter a number of the most learned of the clergy suffered the same fate, including the pious and charitable William Law of King's Cliffe, author of *A Serious Call to a Devout and Holy Life*, who was deprived of his fellowship at Cambridge for his refusal to take the Oath of Abjuration on George I's accession.

However, after the non-jurors, church life in Northamptonshire settled down to a long period of uneventfulness. Disliking 'enthusiasm', the 18th-century parish clergy directed their energy into refuting Calvinism and Rationalism rather than into evangelism and parochial work. In social matters they accepted the *status quo* and looked to an improvement in their station in life. They did not look in vain; Parliamentary Inclosure Acts transformed the parsons' tithes into land, and land values invariably increased after enclosure. In the 18th century many a handsome rectory

109 *The splendid rectory at Ecton, built by Thomas Palmer in 1693.*

was built and the clergy were increasingly recruited from higher up the social scale: at this time the alliance between rectory and big house was cemented in many a Northamptonshire parish. Increasingly sharing the political as well as the social assumptions of the gentry, parsons began to take their place on the magistrates' bench. And by the early 19th century squires who were in holy orders were by no means unusual.

Although never really the religion of the poor, early Dissent belonged to the lower classes more than old Puritanism had done. Information on this and other aspects of the 'heroic age' of nonconformist history in Northamptonshire is revealed in a report made in 1669 by John Palmer, Archdeacon of Northampton. He noted that their 'conventicles' met in barns and private houses in such market towns as Northampton, Daventry and Wellingborough, and certain open villages, such as Long Buckby and Crick, and that the greatest of the meetings was at Kettering, where William Maidwell, the late rector, became the first minister. The archdeacon also noted as 'For their condition there is scarcely any gentleman of £100 per annum that forsakes the Church nor 10 yeomen of that estate that I can find. (Nor) Few men of £50 a year'.[20] Short of men of substance, they were also,

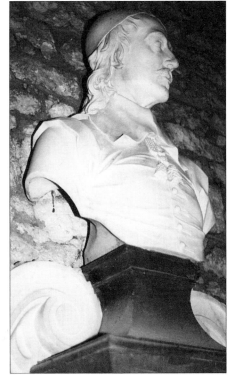

110 *Monument by Rysbrack to Archdeacon John Palmer, rector of Ecton, 1666 to 1680. It was not erected until 1732.*

111 *Independent Chapel, Daventry.*

apparently, low in numbers; the Compton Return of 1676 gave a total for Northamptonshire of only 1,972 'nonconformists' against 83,970 'conformists'. However, there can be little doubt that these early reports overstated the weaknesses of the Northamptonshire Dissenters. The heirs to such a strong tradition would not easily wither away; there was a Puritan hard-core which was irreducible; and survival was as much a matter of quality and temperament as mere numbers. It also had much to do with national politics; neither Charles II, James II, William III, nor the Whig politicians were happy with the religious disabilities imposed by parliament on the nonconformists, and, in fact, by 1689 they had achieved a position of precarious toleration and began to build and open chapels. Their civil disabilities, however, remained; only those who could bend their consciences to accept the Act of Uniformity and the King's Supremacy could take part in politics or enter the professions. Those that could not had perforce to graduate in Scotland, or be satisfied with a life in trade, commerce or industry.

The first achievement of the Dissenters was to weather the early period of persecution; their next was to begin the long 18th-century transformation from a loose network of introspective religious societies into the 'Dissenting Interest'. In this they were led by some very able ministers, the best-known of whom was the Rev. Philip Doddridge (1702-51). From 1730 until his death Doddridge was the minister of the Independent congregation at Castle Hill, Northampton, and there established the reputation which has given him an honoured place in the history of English religion. He was, first of all, a remarkable teacher who played a major part in raising the intellectual level of the Independents. When he moved to Northampton from Kibworth in Leicestershire he brought with him the Academy of which he was the principal. Primarily responsible for the training of young men for the ministry, the Dissenting Academies became notable under Doddridge and others for bringing an almost Scottish rigour to the higher education of Dissenters. After his death the Academy moved to Daventry where it was carried on until 1789.

112 *Northampton's most distinguished Nonconformist, Philip Doddridge, minister of Castle Hill Independent Chapel, 1729 to 1751.*

In addition to his pastoral duties and teaching, Doddridge, despite poor health, found time to write books and tracts, compose hymns and also play an active part in the affairs of his town and his Connection. His most famous works were *The Rise and Progress of Religion in the Soul*, and the important *Free Thoughts on the Most Probable*

Way of Reviving the Dissenting Interest, by a Minister in the Country, which urged the strengthening and unifying of nonconformity. He became a well-known and respected figure in Northampton through his preaching, piety and charitable works. And when proceeded against in the Consistory Court by the curate of Kingsthorpe, fought his case so tenaciously that in the end the king himself intervened to stop further action in the Courts. It was an important test case; thereafter Dissenters were practically safe from

113 *Castle Hill Congregational Church, Northampton, 1695, enlarged in 1862.*

such interference. It is said of Doddridge that he did more than any man to obliterate old party lines and unite nonconformists on a common religious ground. But he did more than that: he allowed into his pulpit both the Methodist John Wesley and the Calvinist Whitefield, and is remembered with them as one of the founders of the Evangelical Revival.

In the two generations after Doddridge the Baptists underwent a similar revival and transformation under the influence of two Northamptonshire ministers, the Rev. John Ryland (1732-92) and the Rev. Andrew Fuller (1754-1815). Ryland, for 25 years minister at College Street chapel in Northampton, was an able preacher and theologian. Through the school he ran in addition to his pastoral duties, he, perhaps more than any minister of his day, preserved the tradition of sound scholarship among the Baptists. Similarly, impor-

114 *The Rev Dr. John Ryland (1732-92), Baptist minister of College Street Chapel, Northampton.*

tant work was done at Kettering, the stronghold of the Northamptonshire Baptists, by Andrew Fuller, minister there from 1782 until his death. Through such works as *The Gospel Worthy of all Acceptation*, reflecting his belief that 'Christ died for all men and not only the elect', Fuller did much to turn the Baptists away from a disputatious over-concentration on Calvinism, towards a more evangelical form of Christianity.

One outcome of this strain of liberal evangelical nonconformity in Northamptonshire was the establishment of protestant overseas missions. In 1792, William Carey (1761-1834), a Baptist shoemaker and later a missionary, Andrew

115 *Walgrave Baptist Chapel, 1786.*

Fuller, Dr. Ryland and others founded the Baptist Missionary Society at an historic meeting in Kettering. It was an important new step; at that time, with the exception of the Moravian brothers, general missionary enterprise was unknown to Protestantism. Yet, in the next half century or so, a remarkable number of men left Northamptonshire to work in the mission fields of the Empire. The most famous were Carey himself, called by the Victorians 'the Wycliffe of India' because of his immense labours in translating the Bible into the languages of the sub-continent, and William Knibb from Kettering, 'Knibb the Notorious', who took up the cause of the slaves in the Jamaica Revolt in 1831.

The Evangelical revival was not, of course, solely the work of the Old Dissenters. John Wesley (who always acknowledged his debt to William Law's *Serious Call*) made at least six visits to the county down to 1780, and after his death Wesleyanism took root. However, it did not play such a central role in religious developments in Northamptonshire as in some other parts of the country, partly because of the revival of Old Dissent, and partly because the county did not suffer the same social dislocation of rapid industrial and urban growth which gave the Wesleyans such opportunities elsewhere. Nevertheless, in the early 19th century the movement had considerable success in Northamptonshire, not least because, of all the denominations, it was the one in which the humbler sort of people felt at home. Its period of greatest growth, however, came later than that of the Old Dissenters, in the second half of the century, so that by 1900 there were rather more Wesleyan and Methodist churches than Baptist and Congregational. Among the beneficed clergy of the Established Church there were a few, such as the Rev. William Hervey (1714-58) of Weston Favell and Collingtree and Thomas Hartley (1709-84) of Winwick, who have a place in the history of the early Evangelical movement, but most of the 18th-century clergy were not of that temper. Nevertheless, in the later 18th and early 19th centuries Sunday Schools, Bible Societies, and a county branch of the National Schools Society were founded, and by then the Church had also begun to move more towards Vital Religion.

116 *Fuller Baptist Church, Kettering. The chapel was renamed 'Fuller' in honour of its most famous minister, after it was rebuilt with a Classical façade in 1861-2.*

The long-term failure of the late 17th-century imposition of religious uniformity was underlined by the 1851 Religious Census, and there were few areas where it failed as demonstrably as Northamptonshire. In 1851 the Church had 292 places of worship with a total of 92,739 sittings; the Independents and Baptists combined had about half as many, with 143 chapels and 41,377 sittings. Taken, however, with the Methodists, with whom they allied on certain religious and political questions of the day, the Protestant Dissenters were almost as numerous as the Church of England, at least in mere numbers of places. The Church, of course, had the advantage of comprehensiveness, of being in every parish, whilst the Dissenters were confined to certain ancient strong places. And the Church had richer supporters to call upon when it came to respond to the many challenges to it in the years after 1851. Yet the most remarkable fact revealed in the census remains the strength of the Baptists and Congregationalists; Northamptonshire was one of the three or four 'Cromwell counties' where Old Dissent, and the even older strain of Puritanism behind it, revealed the depth of their roots. The census also showed Northamptonshire, with its six chapels and 705 sittings, as one of the least Catholic of English counties, though Catholicism was to spread and grow as Northamptonshire industrialised in the second half of the century.

Work, Poverty and the Poor Laws

In the late 18th century many parts of the North and Midlands began to be transformed by the Industrial Revolution. Northamptonshire, by contrast, was almost totally by-passed by it. The first machine to be used in its staple trade was not introduced until 1857, and footwear did not become a factory industry until the 1890s. The steam-engine played virtually no part at all in the county's history; and Northamptonshire did not experience the effects of large-scale growth of towns in the later 18th or early 19th centuries.

There can be little doubt that if coal had been found the story would have been different. Capital would have been drawn in from outside, new industries would have been established, and the landowners converted from opponents of canal and railway developments into supporters of economic change. As it was, local capital in the 18th century was very largely tied up in land, in turnpike trusts (with a vested interest in opposing canals and railways), and in specialist farming for the London market. The increase in output of the footwear industry which began in the last

117 1836 engraving of a painting, 'The Rev W. Carey DD. and his Brahmin Pundit'. Carey, who started life as a Northamptonshire shoemaker, became a Baptist missionary in Bengal and gained fame as 'the Wycliffe of India' for his immense labours translating the Bible into the native languages. In this he was assisted by a Brahmin scholar.

118 *18th-century wool-
comber at work.*

119 *Notice in the
Northampton Mercury
about the yarn market in
Kettering, 1796.*

years of the 18th century was accomplished not by machinery, but by
simply increasing the workforce and introducing some division of labour
into the traditional shoemaking processes. Not needing expensive plant
and machinery, the early manufacturers often set up in business with
relatively little capital.

Reflecting on Northamptonshire's history in the previous century in
an article in the *Quarterly Review* in 1857, the Rev. Thomas James
observed that in the middle of the 18th century 'the weavers of serges,
tammies and shalloons were more numerous than the shoemakers of the
present day'. Remarkable as this statement seems at first sight, it was
correct. Of the 12,000 or so men in the county listed for militia service
in 1777, 12 per cent were weavers or other textile workers, whilst only
half that number were shoemakers.[21] In the later Middle Ages the once-
important Northampton cloth industry had fallen into decline, and had
become extinct in the Tudor period, and the trade at that time never
established itself at all in the rural districts. It was not until the last third
of the 17th century that worsted making was re-introduced into Northamptonshire, specifically as a means of providing employment for the
growing numbers of rural poor, and remained quite a large-scale trade
for rather more than a century. In 1777 the main concentrations of
weavers were at Kettering (the centre of the trade) and at Rothwell,
Northampton, Crick, Welford, Desborough, Corby and Peterborough.
There were also some weavers at Kilsby, Barby, Braunston and West
Haddon. Woolcombing was largely the speciality of Long Buckby and
Kettering, whilst spinning, the work of women, was extensively carried
on in both the weaving, and neighbouring non-weaving, villages.

At this time, farming was, and long remained, the most extensive
employer of labour; in the militia lists in 1777, 51 per cent of the men
worked on the land. Nevertheless, the existence of the worsted trade
was, at a time of population expansion, a most valuable alternative
source of employment. And there were others: in the early 18th century
there was some framework knitting,
though by 1777 this had shrunk to
two or three villages only. At this
time, too, lace-making became an
extensive cottage industry, concentrated in Wellingborough, Northampton and Towcester, and the villages around them. And twice
Northampton attempted to become
a centre of cotton-spinning, though
neither the enterprise of 1743-64,
nor that of 1797-1806 was very successful. In 1791 the trade was
started at Burton Latimer, but the
mill there eventually went over to
carpet and worsted weaving. A few

The COTTON Mill *on the river* Nen; *anciently* Marvel's Mill, *or* Marvelous Mills. *In* 1742 *the Corn-mill was taken down and a new building erected to contain several machines, each having* 50 *spindles for spinning of Cotton, in which near* 100 *children and other hands have been daily employed*.
1. St Peters *steeple.* 2. *A house with a Copper for boiling lye.* 3. *The top of* All Saints *steeple.*
4. *A whitening ground.* 5. St Sepulchres *spire.* 6. *A smiths shop for making the iron work to the spindles*

120 *Illustration of the 18th-century cotton mill in Northampton on Jefferys' map of the town in 1747.*

places developed local specialities—wood-turning at King's Cliffe, whip-making at Daventry, charcoal-burning in the woods at Rockingham—but as employers of people in any numbers these were insignificant. At the time when the Industrial Revolution was getting under way on the coalfields, Northamptonshire men were still employed chiefly on the land, whilst some were weavers, and rather fewer made shoes.

Although Northamptonshire was missed by the main features of the Industrial Revolution it was profoundly affected by one important force which did much to change traditional England at that time; the growth of population from about 1760. What the order of the growth of Northamptonshire's population was between 1760 and 1800 we do not know, no statistics being available before the first census of 1801. However, between 1801 and 1851, a period of very slow economic growth, the county's population grew by 61 per cent (from 132,000 to 212,000), and in the years 1851 to 1901, when the shoe trade underwent its great expansion, it grew to 336,000, a further increase of 93 per cent. This demographic experience is the fundamental fact in the county's (and country's) economic and social history from about 1760. At both the local and the national level it raised the spectre of increasing poverty and poor-rates, and the relationship of employment to population became of crucial importance.

Down to about 1793 it seems that the growth of rural industry in Northamptonshire generally kept pace with the increase in the population. Overall, the expenditure on the maintenance of the poor increased, and there were certain years of crisis, caused by harvest failures, severe winters, or outbreaks of the smallpox, when there was much privation among the poor. Nevertheless, these occasions were accepted as a fact

NORTHAMPTON.

AT a Meeting of the Inhabitants of the Town of NORTHAMPTON, held at the Guildhall in the said Town, the 19th Day of February, 1796, for reducing the present high Price of BUTTER, and adopting Measures for reducing the Price thereof,

(THOMAS HALL, Esq. Mayor, in the Chair.)

It being the Opinion of this Meeting, that the most effectual Method for reducing the present exorbitant Price of Butter, will be to enter into an Engagement, not to purchase that Article at any Rate exceeding Eleven-pence per Pound. It is therefore Resolved, and we whose Names are here-under written do Agree, not to purchase any Butter either in the Market or elsewhere, previous to the 25th Day of March next, at a higher Rate or Price than Eleven-pence a Pound.

RESOLVED, That it be recommended to the Inhabitants to reduce the Consumption of Butter in their respective Families as much as possible.

RESOLVED, That this Meeting will consider themselves as singularly obliged if the Magistrates, or other Chief Officers of the several other Corporate and Market Towns, within this County, will adopt similar Measures to the above, for reducing the Price of Butter, within their respective Districts ; and that the above Resolution be signed by the Chairman, and advertized in the Northampton Mercury.

THOMAS HALL., Chairman.

121 *Notice in the Northampton Mercury in 1796 about the high price of butter.*

of life in pre-Industrial England, and there was no widespread fear that poverty was rising faster than employment. In the 1790s the situation in Northamptonshire took a radical turn for the worse. In the face of the competition from the mechanised textile industry of the West Riding of Yorkshire worsted weaving in many of the other parts of England fell into decline, and in Northamptonshire collapsed almost overnight. The problem was made worse by the fact that this development coincided with a period of economic hardship nationally during the wars against Napoleon and their aftermath. In those years, at a time when bread was the staple food of the poor, the average price of wheat doubled as a result of harvest failures and from supplies from abroad being cut off by the blockade. Between about 1794 and 1834 'the state of the poor' became one of the main questions of English politics.

It was a question which had two essential aspects: the plight of the poor, and the state of mind of those who had to pay taxes for the relief of the poor. In Northampton-shire the plight of the poor was most acute in the former worsted weaving centres. From about 1794 places such as Kettering and Long Buckby were full of half-starved handloom weavers and woolcombers, and their sufferings lasted for nearly two generations. The problem was that no trade came along to replace weaving as an alternative occupation for the poor. It is true that from about 1820 silk-weaving was introduced into Kettering, Desborough and Rothwell. It is also true that in the latter years of the 18th century wholesale shoemaking began to spread out from Northampton into the neighbouring towns and villages. Unfortunately, footwear and silk weaving together did not, in the years of privation down to the 1830s, offer enough jobs to employ all the former weavers and their families. Eventually places such as Kettering, Desborough and Long Buckby did become shoemaking centres, but there was a critical time-lag between the decay of weaving and the expansion of shoemaking.

The other aspect of the crisis was the problem of relieving the poor. Under the Old Poor Law the ratepayers of each parish were solely responsible for their own poor. Even in places such as Kettering, where paupers were so numerous that the ratepayers faced being overwhelmed by the costs of relief, aid from outside was not forthcoming. At this time the parish overseers cast about desperately for ways of reducing the costs of relief. But such commonly-tried devices as setting up parish workhouses, putting the 'able-bodied' to work on the roads, the 'roundsman' system, and supplementing low wages on a scale based on the price of bread (the so-called Speenhamland System) never really worked. In the early 19th century the relief of poverty grew into a political issue, and the southern counties where rural poverty was acute looked to Parliament to reform the Old Poor Law. The tragedy was that the authorities and their Utilitarian 'experts' failed to see the realities of poverty and its causes. Instead they concluded that poverty was in great measure caused by the corruption of the old parish relief system (which undoubtedly had its faults) and the effects this allegedly had in encouraging 'malingerers'.

122 *St Edmund's Hospital, Northampton, the Union Workhouse from 1838 to 1929.*

In the end the Whigs introduced the Poor Law Amendment Act of 1834, which took the management of the relief of poverty away from individual parishes. Parishes were grouped into Poor Law Unions (of which there were 12 in Northamptonshire); Boards of Guardians were elected by the ratepayers, and a workhouse was built in each union. The threat of the workhouse was used as a deterrent to force the poor to do all they could to avoid seeking relief from the Guardians, to separate those 'genuinely in need of relief' from 'able bodied' paupers. This did not reduce the incidence of poverty and, for all that the rules changed, many of the practices of the old system remained. But the new was harsher than the old, and was a source of deep resentment to the labouring classes.

The New Poor Law was an important development in English government. It is often seen as the first step in the growth of the modern bureaucratic state, which it undoubtedly was. Following from this it has been argued that it was a defeat for the local magnates by the forces of centralisation. Nothing could be further from the truth. Steered through parliament by Lord Althorp, later the 3rd Earl Spencer, it was tailor-made to allow them to extend and tighten their control over the countryside. In Northamptonshire it has been shown that the boundaries of the new unions were drawn up to follow very closely the estates of the great landowners; the Brixworth Union was Earl Spencer's; Brackley was the

Cartwrights'; Towcester the Duke of Grafton's; and so on. And, for all their concern with 'economy', the new Boards of Guardians spent lavishly on new workhouses, a surprising fact until one accepts that the New Poor Law was above all designed for the large landowners to extend social control over 'their' parishes. Nothing symbolised more clearly the reality of this control than the new Union Workhouses. They were destined to have a long life; at Northampton, Daventry, Kettering and other places they are still used as hospitals, though the New Poor Law has long been dismantled.

Enclosing the Landscape

In 1750 Northamptonshire was predominantly open-field country. A century later open-field cultivation had virtually all gone; it had been ended, parish by parish, by local Acts of Parliament, mainly in the years between 1760 and 1792. Indeed, so much of Northamptonshire was enclosed by this method the county might serve as a textbook example of the Parliamentary Inclosure movement.

Traditionally the land was worked in two ways—in 'common' and 'in severalty'. Since the time of the Anglo-Saxons, the land in Northamptonshire had been cultivated in common and the system was one in which the holdings of the farmers, their 'yard-lands', lay intermixed in massive open fields. In fact, in most parishes there was only one enormous field divided for the purpose of crop rotation. Naseby field in 1792 was, for instance, divided 'into three parts, not by fences, but by marks made on the ground, called field-marks, so that there may be said to be three fields, viz., one, wheat, rye and barley; one, beans and oats; and one

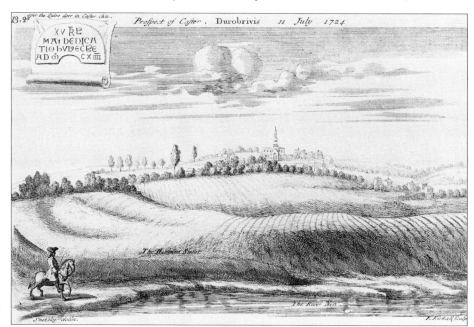

123 *Before enclosure: William Stukeley's engraving of Castor in 1724. A landscape without many hedges or trees.*

fallow'. As on modern allotments, individual plots were divided from one another not by fences or hedges, but by grass boundaries. The essence of such farming was co-operation. The individual had to abide by group decisions as to cultivation and grazing arrived at in the manorial court, and the court officers had the power to fine breakers of its bye-laws, or to impound their stock. It was a system in which tradition and custom were very strong, and in which the preservation of fertility of the land was paramount. Yet it had drawbacks, which came under increasing criticism in the 18th century. It was essentially conservative; 'A man ever so ingenious in agriculture, hath no opportunity of displaying his abilities at Naseby', wrote the vicar there in 1792. 'He is confined to old customs, and can only do the same thing as his neighbours.'[22] New crops were slow to be taken up, and new developments, such as improved drainage, were often ignored. Above all, farming in common was wasteful of time and energy, used up travelling from village farmhouse to plots scattered about the open fields.

Rowell, Northamptonshire.—Freehold Estates.
To be S O L D by A U C T I O N,
By Mr. KIRSHAW,

At the House of Mr. Roe, the Sign of the Sun, in Rowell, in the County of Northampton, on Thursday the 24th Day of September, 1812, at Three o'Clock in the Afternoon, in the following Lots:

Lot 1. ALL those several Pieces or Parcels of ARABLE, MEADOW, and PASTURE LAND, with the Commons and Appurtenances thereunto belonging, situate and being dispersedly in the open and common Fields of ROWELL aforesaid, called Half a Yard Land, or the Sixth Part of Three Yard Lands, and containing by Admeasurement 14 Acres, or thereabouts.

Lot 2. Another HALF YARD LAND, or the Sixth Part of Three Yard Lands, containing the same Quantity, with the usual Right of Common.

Lot 3. Another HALF YARD LAND, or the Sixth Part of Three Yard Lands, containing the same Quantity, with the same Right of Common.

Lot 4. Another HALF YARD LAND, or the Sixth Part of Three Yard Lands, containing the same Quantity, and the same Right of Common.

Lot 5. Another HALF YARD LAND, or the Sixth Part of Three Yard Lands, containing the same Quantity, and the same Right of Common.

Lot 6 Another HALF YARD LAND, or the Sixth Part of Three Yard Lands, containing the same Quantity, and the same Right of Common.

The above Estates are now in the Occupation of Mr. ——— Tongue, Butcher, who will shew the same.

An Act having passed in the last Session of Parliament for inclosing the open Fields of Rowell, the above Lots will be found a most desirable Purchase for any Gentleman who wishes to realize the Property, or to any Persons who may be desirous to increase their Allotments in the said Fields.

For further Particulars, apply to Mr. Howes, Solicitor, or the Auctioneer, in Northampton.

124 *Advertisement in the* Northampton Mercury *in 1812 showing how open-field land at Rothwell was referred to (in yardlands) on the eve of a Parliamentary Inclosure.*

Farming in severalty, that is individually, in the modern manner, was its antithesis, and could only be carried on on inclosed land. As we have seen, inclosures had proceeded in a piecemeal way in Northamptonshire since the Middle Ages, particularly on the estates of the gentry. It was now to be speeded up, and made universal. An important reason for this rapid encrease of inclosure in the second half of the 18th century lay with the rising demand for food, behind which was the inexorable increase in the population. Another was the rise of interest in agricultural improvement, which developed in the reign of George III, whose advocates argued the case for enclosure as an essential preliminary to improved husbandry. In the rapid extension of enclosure the most influential people were the landowners. It was they, not farmers, who promoted it. Before 1750 it had been carried out either by individuals enclosing their estates, or by groups of freeholders agreeing to do so, having the agreement ratified in the Court of Chancery or the Exchequer. In wanting to quicken the process it was natural for the 'landed interest' to turn

A N

A   C   T

F O R

Dividing and Inclofing the Open and Common Fields, Common Paftures, Common Meadows, Common Grounds, and Commonable Lands within the Parifh and Liberties of *Watford*, and within the Hamlet and Liberties of *Murcott*, in the Parifhes of *Watford* and *Long Buckby*, in the County of *Northampton*.

Prefs   **WHEREAS** there are within the Parifh and Li- Preamble.
1   berties of *Watford*, and within the Hamlet and
            Liberties of *Murcott*, in the Parifhes of *Watford*
            and *Long Buckby*, in the County of *Northampton*,
            certain open and common Fields, common Paf-
            tures, common Meadows, common Grounds, and
            commonable Lands, containing together in the
Whole about One thoufand Two hundred and Fifty Acres:

And whereas the King's moft Excellent Majefty, in Right of his Crown of *Great Britain*, is feifed of and in the perpetual Advowfon, Right of Patronage and Prefentation of, in, and to the Vicarage of the Parifh Church of *Watford* aforefaid:

A   **And**

125 *First page of the Act for the Enclosure of Watford, 1771.*

to parliament. Of the 234 parishes enclosed in Northamptonshire after 1749 all but one were enclosed by Act of Parliament; of the 76 or so before that date, only one had been enclosed by this method. The incentive to landowners to inclose was not only to improve husbandry; they were spurred on by the profit-motive. Inclosure invariably increased land values, and therefore rents. It was for these reasons that the larger freeholders were prepared to bear the heavy costs of getting an Act through parliament, and of surveying, hedging, draining and road-making when an Inclosure Award was implemented.

These reasons did not usually appear in the wording of an Inclosure Act. Usually only two were given. The first outlined the disadvantages of the open-field system. In the words of the Daventry Act of 1802, 'The Lands of the owners or proprietors ... are intermixed and disposed of in small parcels in the fields, and in their present state of cultivation are incapable of improvement, and it would be advantageous to owners to have the same divided and inclosed and allotted according to their rights'. The objective was to gather together the scattered property of the landowners so that it could then be divided into modern 'ring-fence' farms, and the tenant farmers could abandon farming in common and begin farming in severalty. The other objective usually specified in an Act was the abolition of tithe, and the compensation of the holder of the tithes for his loss with a grant of land in the Inclosure Award. This award in lieu was often very valuable, amounting in the early 19th century usually to one-fifth of the arable and one-ninth of the rest of the land of the manor. The owner, or 'impropriator', of the tithes was not always a clergyman, but the objective of the abolition of tithe in a Parliamentary Inclosure Award was to improve the position of the Church of England in the countryside, at the same time as removing a long-standing grievance of farmers. This, no doubt, was one reason why parsons were often numbered among the most earnest advocates of enclosure.

The Inclosure Act appointed a body of Commissioners, usually country gentlemen, estate stewards, or surveyors, not having a direct interest in the particular parish to be enclosed, who took an oath to carry out the process fairly. They then met a number of times in the village, heard claims from landowners and claimants of common rights, and in due course produced an Award. What they did in effect was to gather in all the scattered pieces of property and re-allocate them to those with proveable legal claims, with an eye not only to quantity of land but also to quality. Often there followed some private exchanges of land between landowners so that as far as possible each could gather his property into discrete units, so that it could be let out as ring-fence farms.

126   *Hedger's axe.*

The end of open-field farming and the extinguishing of common rights killed an ancient way of life, and was something of a revolution. It removed the need for farmers to co-operate closely with one another and, as their new farmhouses were often built away from the villages, they became physically more separate from their neighbours. Having lost their most important functions (the regulation of the open-fields) the manorial courts fell into decline as organs of village government. The common people lost their right to roam freely over the land of their native parish, though they obstinately continued to use ancient footpaths, despite attempts to close-off rights of way. The landscape of Northamptonshire was transformed: in place of the vast open fields relatively small inclosures were made, bounded by straight lines of quicksets, and trees were not only planted in these hedges, but in coverts, partly to improve the scenery and provide shade, partly to encourage game.

Enclosure satisfied all the people who mattered in rural society—the larger landowners, the parsons and farmers. It satisfied landowners because land values rose, the heavy initial outlay being regarded as capital investment, which, indeed, is what it was. These charges, however, were often too high for smaller freeholders, and they often sold out on the eve of an enclosure. There was a tendency therefore for the process to concentrate land into fewer hands. Parsons not infrequently had the pleasure of seeing their stipends augmented, and many a fine parsonage was built in the years following an enclosure. The laying out of ring-fence farms generally pleased the farmers. Released from the wasted energy, irritations, and innate conservatism of the open-field system they were free to farm as they pleased.

But what of the labourers? It is widely believed that Parliamentary Inclosure robbed the poor of customary rights and thereby worsened their lot, that it was deeply resented by them, that it increased rural poverty and forced labourers and their families off the land. There is little doubt that the time of the enclosures was a time when the situation of the agricultural labourer worsened. By the time it was complete he was lucky if he had any means of sustenance between him and the workhouse except his day wages. By no means all cottages had gardens,

127   *'Agricultural Gates', Holly Lodge, Boughton.*

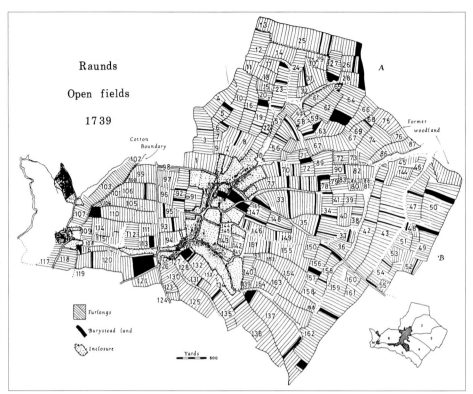

128 *D.N. Hall's map of Raunds before enclosure. There were six great fields divided for the most part into the lands and furlongs of the arable. The areas marked A and B were late Saxon woodland later incorporated into the open fields.*

and the call for allotments for labourers was largely resisted until the 1880s. This 'proletarianisation' of the labourers had, however, been going on for centuries, and the Parliamentary Inclosure era was the last act and finale to an ancient process. In the strictly legal sense enclosure by commissioners was not expropriation. Those with legal rights were compensated in the award and it is not usually suggested that commissioners acted dishonestly. The question of cottage rights, too, is sometimes misunderstood. By no means all cottages in a village carried common rights, especially in open villages which had grown large since the Middle Ages. Nevertheless the right to graze a cow or pig on the waste or common was often of importance in the economy of the poor, and there is no doubt that landowners and farmers had an interest (which they openly admitted) in removing the last vestiges of economic independence the labourer had, which is why in the 19th century they generally opposed allotments. The enclosure movement completed this process, and was long resented for that reason.

Outward manifestations of this resentment are, however, hard to find in Northamptonshire. In 1764 there was a riot over enclosure at West Haddon, and the cottagers at Raunds (an open village) petitioned parliament against the loss of their common rights in 1797. However, an important point in all this is that enclosure cannot be taken in isolation from other contemporary developments impinging on rural life. Rising

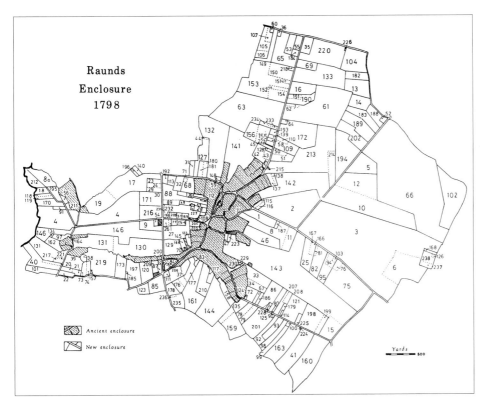

Raunds
Enclosure
1798

Ancient enclosure
New enclosure

Yards 500

129 *D.N. Hall's map of Raunds after enclosure in 1798. The unhedged furlongs of the open fields have now been re-allotted in blocks and divided by straight-sided hedges, creating the present pattern on the face of the land.*

poor rates and unemployment were caused more by the general rise in population and the collapse of rural industry than by enclosure, a fact which a few contemporary observers grasped, at least in part. Writing of Naseby in 1792 (then still open-field) the Rev. John Mastin noted the increase in poor rates following the decline of worsted-weaving and spinning, and pointed out, 'Inclosures have been condemned for having this bad effect, but the above is demonstrative proof they are not always the cause; they have risen here as rapidly in proportion as in inclosed lordships, and are sure to be found high in every place where manufactories are carried on'.[23]

Whatever the particular causes, the situation of the labourers in the late 18th and early 19th centuries was certainly bad and getting worse. Contrary to popular belief, they did not migrate in large numbers from the land following enclosure, but stuck it out. There was, of course, a steady migration of people from the county both to English towns and to America for economic reasons at this time, as there had been for religious reasons in the 17th century. But the mass exodus from the land did not begin in Northamptonshire until as late as the 1870s. In the late enclosure era social tensions were reflected by such events as the 'Swing' riots in 1830, and by outbreaks of crimes (particularly arson) against the property of farmers in times of privation. It was because of these that the county police and the harsh New Poor Law were introduced in the 1830s.

130 *Detail of doorway, Corn Exchange, Thrapston.*

131 *Thorplands farm, Northampton, early 19th century.*

However, in Northamptonshire privation was never quite so acute nor social tensions so sharp, as in some of the southern counties, the principal reason being that shoemaking spread slowly into many of the villages in the early 19th century.

Farming after Enclosure

Between about 1800, the peak of the Parliamentary Inclosure movement, and the outbreak of the Great War in 1914, agriculture in Northamptonshire can be said to have passed through four phases: the period down to the end of the Napoleonic Wars in 1815; the era of the Corn Laws; the years of 'High Farming' between 1846 and 1874; and the Great Agricultural Depression and its aftermath between 1874 and 1914.

It is a common misconception to link enclosure with the rise of scientific farming. The former, a piecemeal process, took place one, two, or sometimes three, generations before the latter got under way in the mid-Victorian years. Yet if the improvements introduced into farming as a direct result of enclosure were relatively simple and unscientific, they were nevertheless very important. Ring-fence farming reduced wasted effort; the new, smaller fields made for better controlled grazing; the spread of up-and-down husbandry in the place of three- or four-field rotation, the abolition of commons, and the taking in of the waste made it relatively easy to increase the acreage of land under cultivation. As a result output could be, and was, significantly increased without any very important technical advances.

And at that time it was necessary to increase output, first of all to meet the demand for food from a rising population, and then to feed the nation during the long struggle against the French between 1793 and

132 *Naseby after enclosure in 1820: a hedged landscape, created on a drawing board by an enclosure surveyor.*

1815, when European sources of wheat were cut off. There is much that is uncertain about the history of farming in this period, but it is clear that land that had long been under grass was ploughed up for cereals, and much marginal land cultivated. Whatever the sufferings of the rural poor, farmers did well, wheat prices roughly doubling in this period, and many observers remarked on the rise in their standard of living.

It is not surprising that after the French Wars ended they wanted the good times to go on. Parliament, dominated by the landed interest, gave them the protection of the Corn Laws, which excluded foreign wheat until the price of British wheat rose to a specified level. In the 1820s this policy attracted the opposition of economists, Radical politicians and the new manufacturers in the North. From 1838 the Anti Corn-Law League, a powerful pressure group organised in Manchester, challenged this 'dear bread' policy. Interested in Free Trade and low-wage costs as well as cheap food, the rich and well-organised League thoroughly alarmed the Protectionist farmers of Northamptonshire, who looked to the Tory party to resist. This struggle dominated county politics in the early Victorian period, particularly when the Whig grandees announced their conversion to Free Trade. In 1846 the farmers and the Tory party were thrown into confusion when Peel's Conservative government, faced with the Irish famine, repealed the Corn Laws.

Dire ruin was predicted by the farming community, forseeing a flood of cheap foreign produce pouring into this county. In fact, a generation of remarkable prosperity and progress followed. If Northamptonshire was a prominent cereals area it also continued to remain a major producer of wool and meat. 'The general richness of the soil makes it particularly favourable to grazing, for which it is now famous', the Rev. Thomas James observed in the *Quarterly Review* in 1857. 'Beasts are bought in the spring from the droves

FARMERS!

Listen to Reason; don't be humbugged by the Placards that are issued to divert your attention. Stick to the CORN LAWS though Lord Milton avoids them. He has repeatedly said Five Shillings per Bushel is plenty for Wheat. With that idea what protection can you expect from him, if he could alter the present Corn Laws to a fixed duty.

He would give a duty which would lower Wheat to Forty Shillings per Quarter. But he has also said, if his plan was adopted in the manner he should wish, Corn should be imported *free* of Duty.

Pledges are demanded from the Candidates in the Manufacturing Districts, whose game Lord Milton is playing, that they will support a total repeal of the Corn Laws. Lord Milton is ready to support the party who advocate the Abolition of the Corn Laws.

Farmers in the name of common sense, send him to his own Borough of Malton; don't let him represent an Agricultural County.

DASH, PRINTER, KETTERING.

133 *An anxious Tory Protectionist handbill from the election for North Northamptonshire in 1832. The Whig Lord Milton was suspected (correctly as it happened) of being a Free-trader.*

134 *A breeder of prize Leicester sheep, Valentine Barford, of Foscote, near Towcester. His subscription portrait by Henry Barraud was paid for by his customers (or friends as he preferred to call them) in 1857.*

W. BUTLIN,
VULCAN WORKS, NORTHAMPTON.

W. B. begs to inform his Friends and the Public generally that he continues to Manufacture his Portable STEAM ENGINES, which are celebrated for their Stability and Economy. They are more durable, require fewer fire boxes, and are less liable to leaky tubes than most makers.
A List of Prices sent upon application to the Works.

W. BUTLIN,
AGENT FOR MESSRS. P. & H. P. GIBBONS'S
STEAM THRASHING MACHINES.

THE above (No. 1) is an illustration of their Finishing Machine (to be driven by a six or seven-horse power engine) for preparing the corn fit for market in one operation; it is fitted with Goucher's patent beaters, thrash clean without breaking the corn, also a patent revolving screen, which makes a perfect separation. It has lately undergone many important improvements, which renders it the most simple, durable and effective Machine ever introduced to the public. Every part is easy of access for repairs, and the style of workmanship cannot be surpassed. Price £112.
No. 2, same as above (without Dressing Apparatus), price £95; to be driven by a five or six-horse engine.
No. 3 is a Machine adapted for all kinds of grain, to be driven by a four-horse engine; it is four feet in width, fitted with straw shakers, elevators, barley hummeller, and two blowers; it is light and compact, well suited for hill districts or small occupiers. Price £82.
No. 4, similar to No. 3, with 3ft. 6in. drum, and single blower; to be driven by a three-horse engine. Price £60; Barley Horner, £5 extra.
W. B. can with confidence recommend these Machines for their efficiency, simplicity and durability.

Apply to—
W. BUTLIN,
VULCAN ENGINE WORKS, NORTHAMPTON.

135 *High Farming. An advertisement for W. Butlin's steam engines and thrashing machines in the* Northampton Mercury *in 1860.*

of Devons, Herefords, Scotch, Irish or Welsh cattle which are brought to the fairs and markets, and are fattened off the land, without any artificial food, supplying the London market from July to December, the best being reserved after a little oil-cake for the great Christmas market.' And it transpired that, if tariffs had gone, England still enjoyed the protection of geography: the wide oceans had not yet been tamed by the steamship, and the North American prairies were not yet producing their vast surpluses for export. Rising demand for food from the home market, and the introduction of scientific farming, in the form of fertilisers, deep-draining, machinery, and stock-breeding ushered in the era of 'High Farming'. Books on husbandry became popular, local agricultural societies circulated new ideas, model farms were experimented with, landowners built new cottages for the labourers. Much of this had started before the Repeal of the Corn Laws. The Royal Agricultural Society had been founded in 1837, and the 3rd Earl Spencer, as well as being a leading Whig politician, found time to be its president. He took a pride in being known as 'a farmer among gentlemen and a gentleman among farmers'. However, from about 1850 scientific farming became fashionable. The coming of the railway acted as a stimulus to agricultural distribution, and long-decayed markets, as at Long Buckby and Rothwell, re-opened in the late 1840s (though not for long). In 1866 accurate statistics started to be collected for the first time, revealing that in that year 271,000 acres of Northamptonshire were arable as against 252,000 under grass. The trend towards arable, however, reached its peak just a few years later. It was to be sharply reversed by the Great Depression which began in 1874.

The farmers of Northampton-shire (and elsewhere), long used to good prices for their wheat, were hit by a series of bad harvests, and the dual catastrophe of a prolonged fall in world commodity prices and the entry of cheap produce from North America and Australasia, which began in the 1870s. The result was the 'Agricultural Interest', both landowners and farmers, now suffered what had been predicted when the Corn Laws were repealed. Land values and rents fell, and great numbers of farmers faced bankruptcy. The urban dweller, of course, benefited: with the drop in the price of food living standards rose. The agricultural labourers for the first time began to migrate from the land *en masse.* Pushed by the Depression (which dragged on until 1896), they were also attracted from the villages by better wages in the footwear industry, undergoing great expansion at that time. By 1900 the once-populous countryside had emptied. This period was one of the great discontinuities in the history of Northamptonshire—villages shrank, family names that had been there for generations vanished, rural culture fell into decline. In time adjustments were made, as they had to be. Clearly Northamptonshire farmers had to concentrate more on beef production and dairying, and less on arable farming. By 1914 twice as much land was under grass than under crops.

By 1900 the decline of the countryside had attracted a certain amount of concern, but official policy remained non-interventionist; Britain remained committed to Free Trade. In the Great War of 1914-18 central direction did come in, and there was a reversal of the downward trend in arable farming. Britain's farmers succeeded in feeding the nation through the German U-boat campaign of 1917. But in the inter-war years the old trend to increasing grazing and reducing cereal production was returned to; by 1938-39 69 per cent of the land in Northamptonshire was under grass, while only 20 per cent was arable. Once again in the Second World War there was a hasty reversal of this trend under government direction. And since 1945 governments have stepped in with subsidies to ensure farmers are not so much at the mercy of Free Trade, and there was a significant switch back to arable farming in Northamptonshire. More recently there is the European Common Agricultural Policy designed to support the farming interest.

THE NORTHAMPTONSHIRE
AGRICULTURAL SOCIETY'S SHOW

WILL be held at STAMFORD, on THURSDAY, the 17TH JULY, 1862.
PRESIDENT: The Lord BURGHLEY, M.P.
VICE-PRESIDENT: The Earl of DALKEITH.
PRIZES to the amount of £800 will be awarded.
A GRAND FLOWER SHOW will take place at the Same Time.

A PAVILION DINNER

Will be held in the Park at Four o'clock on the day of Show, and the Committee particularly request that the Ladies will favour them with their attendance, as on previous similar occasions.

For the convenience of Visitors dining and wishing to sit together, the seats will be numbered, and may be secured on application to Mr. H. JOHNSON, St. Mary's-street, Stamford, where a plan may be seen.

GENTLEMEN'S TICKETS, 3s. 6d. LADIES' TICKETS, 2s. 6d.

Members of the Society, who have paid their Subscriptions, will receive a Ticket from the Secretary, to admit them FREE to the Show Yard on Wednesday and Thursday. The Ticket not Transferable.

The Public will be admitted on WEDNESDAY, 16TH JULY, at One o'clock, on payment of 2s. 6d., to witness the trial of Horses, which will take place before the Judges; and also of the other Stock, after the Prizes have been awarded; and on THURSDAY, 17TH, the Show Yard will be opened at Nine o'clock as usual.

ADMISSION—ONE SHILLING EACH.

Entries closed on 1st July.
Any information may be obtained on application to
JOHN M. LOVELL, Secretary.
Harpole, Weedon, July 3rd, 1862.

136 *Advertisement for the County Agricultural Society's Show in 1862.*

137 *Corn Exchange, Northampton, 1850.*

Anno Undecimo

Georgii Regis.

An Act for Enlarging the Term granted by an
Act passed in the Sixth Year of the Reign of
Her late Majesty Queen Anne, Intituled, *An
Act for Repairing the Highways from Old
Stratford in the County of Northampton, to
Dunchurch in the County of Warwick, and for
making the same more effectual.*

138 *Act of Parliament
for the Old Stratford to
Dunchurch Turnpike,
1725.*

Since the Second World War, and particularly recently, a change
has come over rural life which is both quantitative and qualitative. With
the outward spread of towns, the growth of motor-car ownership, and
the general rise in prosperity, people have returned to living in villages
in Northamptonshire, as elsewhere. Rural decline has been arrested, and
rural life, once looked down on, now enjoys high prestige. Where once
the downtrodden labourer lived, the middle classes seek the good life.

Turnpikes and River Navigation

The rise in prosperity of Northamptonshire's economy in the reign of
Queen Elizabeth was, as we have already seen, in large measure the
result of the revival of inland trade. From then until the railway era the
county's fortunes were to be intimately involved with those of the nation's
roads. The improvement of the highways with the introduction of the
turnpikes therefore brought considerable benefits, and the navigation of
the River Nene between 1713 and 1760, connecting Northampton with
the east-coast shipping trade, dove-tailed neatly into this existing pattern
of communications. The development of the canals in the 1790s, and the
later railway system, so important as stimulators of industrial development in certain other regions of England, were not, however, destined to
prove quite so advantageous to Northamptonshire.

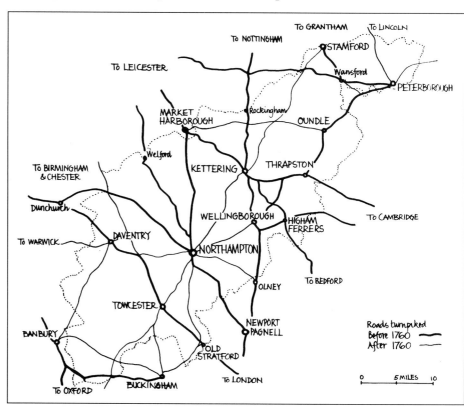

139 *The turnpike roads
of Northamptonshire.*

The first roads in the county to be handed over by Act of Parliament to turnpike trusts for repair, maintenance and improvement were stretches of national trunk roads. The more important the road, the earlier the Act. The first was the Old Stratford to Dunchurch stretch of the great road from London to Chester, which ran through Towcester and Daventry, turnpiked following the Act of 1706. This was followed by the Stoke Goldington to Northampton Act of 1709, and the roads out of Northampton to Leicester were turnpiked in the 1720s. The next was for that part of the Great North Road between Wansford and Stamford, which got its Act in 1748-9. Next legislated for (in the 1750s) came the network of roads passing through Kettering, and by then all the major

140 *A turnpike milepost, formerly at Chapel Brampton, now in the Abington Park Museum, Northampton.*

routes traversing Northamptonshire had been turnpiked. Those subsequently improved in this way were cross-country lines of communication of local, rather than national, significance. It was not until the 1790s that the roads linking Stamford and Brackley (at each end of the county) were turnpiked, and it was not until as late as 1819 that Northampton and Kettering were directly connected by a new turnpike road.

The turnpike trusts which managed the main roads in the 18th and early 19th centuries were important local institutions. Much local capital was tied up in them, for these roads were paid for out of loans secured against the income from the tolls levied on them. The running of the turnpikes was farmed out by the trustees, and turnpike contractors' profits were made from the excess of toll income over what they paid for the contract and their other costs. Although users of the turnpikes grumbled profusely (and with reason) about the state of the roads, and the delays caused by the turnpike gates, there is little doubt that they were an improvement on all previous methods of maintaining the highways. Traffic speeded up. In 1720

On Monday, the 24th of October laft, at Three o'Clock in the Morning, fet out (and will continue fo to do) from the White-Lyon in Northampton,

A Good and Neat Ge-hoe Coach, with fix Able Horfes, (whichwillwithEafe andPleafure carry eightPerfons) andwill be at the Ram Inn in Smithfield, London, every Tuefday early in the Afternoon; returns on Wednefday about Ten o'Clock, and will be in Northampton on Friday Afternoon. Every Paffenger to London paying feven Shillings, and from London to Northampton fix Shillings, being allow'd fourteen Pounds Weight, and for all above as well as for other Goods as ufual.

Perform'd (if God permit) by
ROBERT HERBERT.

Note, Paffengers being ready at Newport-Pagnell by Ten o'Clock, may be taken in there.

Note alfo, Plate, Money, Writings, or Jewels will not be anfwer'd for, unlefs Notice be given thereof.

141 *Advertisement in the* Northampton Mercury, *1743, for the weekly Ge-hoe Coach to and from London.*

Harborough *and* Welford Roads.

IN Purfuance of the Order of Sir Juftinian Iſham, Baronet; William Hanbury, and William Zouth Lucas Ward, Efquires; the Rev. Eufeby Iſham, Langham Rokeby, John Sanford, Charles Marſhall, and William Stanton, Clerks; and Mr. Trefham Chapman:—Notice is hereby given, that the Truftees appointed by Act of Parliament for more effectually amending, widening, and-keeping in Repair, the Turnpike-Roads leading from the Town of Northampton to Chain-Bridge, near the Town-of Market-Harborough; and from the Direction-Poſt in Kingſthorpe, in the County of Northampton, to Welford-Bridge, in the ſaid County, will, on Tuesday the Sixteenth Day of September next, between the Hours of Eleven in the Forenoon and Two in the Afternoon, at the Houfe of Widow Green, the George Inn, at Brixworth, in the faid County, LETT to FARM by AUCTION to the BEST BIDDER or BIDDERS, in the Manner as directed by the Act paffed in the thirteenth Year of His prefent Majefty, for regulating Turnpike Roads, The TOLLS of the GATES or TURNPIKES erected upon the faid Roads, at or near Brixworth-Bridge, Chain-Bridge, Brampton-Bridge, and Thurnby, for one Year, commencing from the fourth Day of December next :—Which faid feveral Tolls produced clear in the laſt Year, the refpective Sums following; at which they will be feparately put up, viz.

Brixworth-Bridge	£ 691
Chain-Bridge	490
Brampton-Bridge	232
Thurnby	124

The beft Bidder or Bidders muft forthwith produce fufficient Sureties, and give Security for Payment of the Monies Monthly or Quarterly, as fhall be required by the Truftees.

And Notice is hereby further given, That all Bills on Account of the faid Roads, are expected to be fent to the Surveyors previous to the Day of Meeting, for the Purpofe of being laid before the Truftees for their Infpection and Examination, and that Orders for Payment of the Monies due thereon may be immediately given.

Dated this fifteenth Day of Auguft, 1788.
J. MARKHAM,
Clerk to the Truftees of the faid Roads.

142 *Letting the tolls on the Harborough and Welford turnpikes, 1788.*

the 'Northampton Flying Waggon' took about 18 hours to reach London: 60 years later stage waggons were doing the journey in twelve.

The period from 1790 to 1840 was the great era of the turnpike roads in Northamptonshire. It was ushered in by a number of developments, the first of which was the rise of the Royal Mail coaches. Before 1784 the mails were carried on horseback, but in that year a system of mail coaches run by stage proprietors under government licence was started. They set a new standard of speed and efficiency, and soon fast stage coaches were competing with them for passengers and parcels, cutting down the times of long-distance journeys. Behind these developments lay advances in coach design, especially springing, and in road making. One of the greatest civil engineers of the period was Thomas Telford, and one of his greatest projects affected the Old Stratford to Dunchurch turnpike in Northamptonshire. Following the Act of Union with Ireland in 1801 the government decided to improve road and ferry communications between London and Dublin. After surveying the route in 1816 Telford was given the task of virtually building a new road from Shrewsbury to Holyhead on Anglesey, and improving the existing one from London to Shrewsbury. As a result, the 1820s saw considerable works on the road through Towcester and Daventry. Telford's work in straightening bends and levelling of gradients can still be seen on the modern A5 in that area. The coaching era reached its peak a few years later in the 1830s. The principal road-towns of Northamptonshire were then alive with the bustle of numerous coaches regularly passing through, the fastest of which were performing the 72 miles or so to and from London in the remarkable time of seven and three quarter hours.

Although the turnpikes improved the roads they had a number

Northampton elegant Light Coach,

Upon an entire new Principle,

For Four Insides, and Three Outsides,

Now offered to the Public by Messrs. Willan *and* Levi, *Proprietors of the Old Northampton Coach,*

WILL commence-on Monday the 25th Instant from Northampton, and from London on Tuesday the 26th; to start precisely at Seven o'Clock in the Morning, and to continue every other Day (till another of the Kind can be provided) as follows:—

From Mr. Levi's Office, *Gold-Street, Northampton,* on *Mondays, Wednesdays,* and *Fridays;* and from the Bull-and-Mouth Inn, *Bull-and-Mouth-Street, London,* on *Tuesdays, Thursdays,* and *Saturdays,* at the same Hour.

☞ To have One Coachman *only* throughout the Journey, and to stop at no Place on the Road, except for the Purpofe of changing Horses; by which Means the Paffengers will arrive in good Time to Dinner.

*** Inside Fare 15s.—and Outside 9s.

N. B. The *Old Coach* every Morning as usual.

London, June 19th, 1804.

143 *Advertisement for the Northampton to London 'elegant Light Coach', 1804.*

of disadvantages. The gates slowed up traffic, the tolls irritated users and pushed up transport costs, and the roads were not always kept in good repair. Above all, it was not nearly as efficient to transport heavy or fragile goods by road as by water.

144 *Politics and River Navigation: commemoration in stone of an aristocratic gift for the improvement of the River Nene.*

In the century from about 1650 many of the rivers of England were improved (or 'navigated') by the straightening of bends and the building of locks round obstacles such as mills. As early as 1662 Thomas Fuller, pointing out what the Dutch had done on their waterways, was urging that the Nene should be made navigable from 'Peterburg to Northampton'. Clearly such a major project would have to be taken in stages. A scheme for improving it as far as Oundle was mooted in 1692, but not carried through until 1730, following Acts of Parliament in 1713 and 1724. Thrapston was reached in 1737, but there, for nearly another twenty years, the Navigation ended. In 1754 the project revived. Another Act of Parliament was secured, the Commissioners of the Western Division of the Nene were constituted, and put the work of navigating the river up to Northampton in the hands of Smith of Attercliffe, in Yorkshire. In 1758-60 he carried it through at a cost of £14,000, giving the river a minimum draught of four feet, and putting in 20 locks, some of which were paid for by local magnates. In the famous 'Three Earls' election at Northampton in 1768 the candidates spent £3,000 on river locks to buy political influence with the electors. The Nene Navigation was an undoubted commercial success, giving a good return for the next eighty years or so on capital invested in it. It fitted nicely with the county's pattern of roads and market towns. Down-river passed much of Northamptonshire's agricultural produce, and up-river came produce from the North-East and Northern Europe—coal, timber, slate and glass.

By the last decade of the 18th century important developments were taking place in the provinces which were to affect the economic future of this country. The Industrial Revolution was transforming Birmingham, Manchester and their regions into great centres of manufacturing. In this period towns on the road to Birmingham, such as Towcester and Daventry, and Northampton, on the road to Manchester, began to feel the effect of this with a marked increase in the volume of traffic. The growing need, however, was to improve the transport of heavy goods between these centres and the capital, and the commercial interest looked to the construction of a canal from Birmingham to London to achieve this. The question was, how would this affect Northamptonshire?

145 *Canal locks at Blis-
worth.*

5

Northamptonshire in the Nineteenth Century

Canals and Railways

A canal from London to Birmingham was potentially of great importance to Northamptonshire. A direct route must pass through the county,
and its benefits seemed obvious, particularly to Northampton, where the
expansion of the wholesale manufacture of footwear was just beginning.
However, in the matter of both canals and railways, the county was to
suffer from the checks geography and geology can impose on the economic ambitions of men.

By 1790 a national canal network had already been created, which
linked the Mersey, Humber, Severn and Thames, with its centre in the
Black Country. However, the weakness in this system was the link between Birmingham and the Thames, which was then via the Birmingham
and Fazeley, and Coventry and Oxford canals. It was narrow gauge,
indirect, and the Thames between Oxford and London was in poor navigable state. In 1792 a scheme was put forward for a 'Grand Junction'
canal from the Oxford canal at Braunston in Northamptonshire to London, and an Act was got through parliament the following year. In the
early days there were some hopes that Northampton might become the
centre of a water-transport network linking Eastern England and the
East Coast trade, via Wisbech and the Nene Navigation, with London,
the Midlands and the North. These were soon dashed. Because of the
topography of the Northampton district, and the great cost of constructing locks into and out of the town, the canal was constructed along a line
passing through Braunston, Long Buckby, Stoke Bruerne and Cosgrove
a few miles to the west. Had Northampton and Daventry been more
important as manufacturing centres these costs might possibly have been
borne by the Canal Company, but the footwear trade had only recently
begun to grow, and neither town even got so much as a branch of the
canal.

If the Canal Company avoided the pitfalls of geography around
Northampton, it encountered those of geology at Blisworth. There a
ridge of land lay athwart the line of the canal and, after trying and
failing between 1793 and 1796 to construct a tunnel through, the company had to admit defeat. A flight of locks over the hill was proposed,
but rejected in favour of a 'plateway' for horse-drawn waggons, until

such time as another tunnel could be constructed. The Grand Junction canal opened for traffic in 1799: until 1805 cargoes from Birmingham were unloaded at Blisworth, and those from London at Stoke Bruerne, to be carted along the plateway and re-loaded into narrow boats to carry on to their destination. A second Blisworth tunnel was eventually constructed between 1802 and 1805 at a cost of £90,000.

As a major artery of trade, for nearly fifty years the canal enjoyed great prosperity. It linked the great London market with the provincial centres of industry, and brought into Northamptonshire cheaper coal, Welsh slate, Staffordshire pottery, and limestone, lime and fertilisers, and carried away the produce of the county. From the time it first opened, Northampton pressed for a branch canal. It was slow in coming—it needed expensive locks, and there was a shortage of water. To appease the town the Canal Company laid a plateway from Gayton wharf to Northampton, using some of the old Blisworth waggonway materials. It was not until 1815 that Northampton got its canal arm. It came at an opportune moment, just as the footwear industry might have faltered in the recession at the end of the Napoleonic Wars. In fact, it did not do so, but continued to expand, and in the 40 years between 1811 and 1851 Northampton's population tripled.

At the same time as the Grand Junction was being planned a canal scheme to link Leicester and Northampton was set in motion. It was part of a scheme to connect the Trent and the Notts-Derby coalfield to the Grand Junction canal. The Act for the Leicester and Northamptonshire Union canal was passed the same day in 1793 as that for the Grand Junction. Again geography, and the relative economic unimportance of Leicester and Northampton at that time, dogged progress. By 1809 the canal had only been constructed as far south as Market Harborough, and was destined never to reach Northampton. It was re-started in 1810, but this time was to run from Foxton to Norton, where it joined the Grand Junction, with an arm to Welford. It came into use in 1814. The

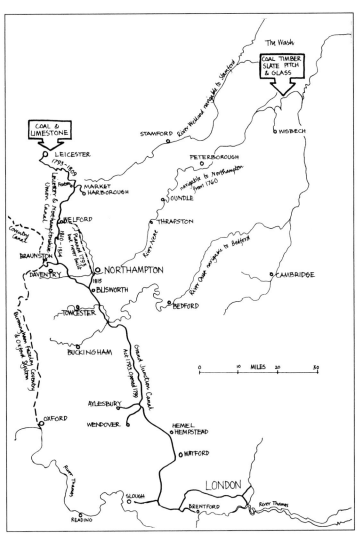

146 *Northamptonshire and the national canal system.*

147 *Canal milepost, Welford.*

148 *The canal at Stoke Bruerne. The warehouse is now a museum.*

149 *Constructing the Kilsby tunnel. J.C. Bourne's sketch of work at one of the entry shafts. This tunnel gave George Stephenson one of his biggest problems in building the London and Birmingham Railway.*

'Union Canal' was never a great commercial success, and the reason lay basically with the fact that Leicester's great industrial expansion did not come until later, in the era of the railways.

When the railway era began, Northampton, as in the 1790s, might well have felt that it was going to benefit directly from the new line of communication between London and Birmingham. But as with the construction of the Grand Junction canal, the town was by-passed when the London and Birmingham railway was planned. A myth, exposed as long ago as the 1930s, but still widely held, grew up that Northampton's Corporation had been foolish enough to oppose the plans to bring the railway through the town. This was not true: there never was any intention on the part of the Company to do so. The gradient into the town was beyond the power of the puny locomotives of the time, and Robert Stephenson was careful to site his line well away from the Spencer estates just outside the town to avoid landowner antagonism as the Bill passed through parliament. It is true that the· Corporation of Northampton was unco-operative over a proposal to cross a Corporation estate at Bugbrooke, and this possibly is the origin of the myth that they opposed the line through the town. It has been suggested that Stephenson later gave credence to this story as a cover for his difficulties constructing the Kilsby tunnel, which he as the engineer should have foreseen. Suggesting that the line would have taken another route but for Northampton's opposition shifted the blame over the expense of the Kilsby tunnel from his shoulders.

The London and Birmingham (soon to become part of the London and North-Western Railway) was one of the busiest of the nation's railways, and from the local point of view it was a great pity it passed through Weedon, Blisworth and Wolverton instead of Northampton. Rugby became what Northampton

X *Shoe factories: Marlows'*
Phoenix Works, St George's Street,
Northampton, built and extended in
the 1890s, burned down in the 1990s.

XI *Shoe factories: Timpsons',*
Kettering, built 1923, closed 1974,
now demolished.

XII *Construction of the new*
Greyfriars bus station, Northamp-
ton, 1974. In the background is the
high rise block of Northampton
House.

XIII *Northampton Development Corporation's map of how Northampton was to be expanded. What the map set out was virtually completed by 1985.*

XIV *Urban renewal in the 1970s. The* Saxon Inn, *Northampton (latterly the* Moat House Hotel*), and surroundings. Behind and to the left is the brutalist Mayorhold multi-storey car park..*

and Daventry would have liked to have been—the Midland junction where important railway works were located. As it was, the railway killed the road traffic through Towcester and Daventry within a matter of weeks of its opening in 1838. From then until very recent times Daventry stagnated, despite having the footwear industry. In the Victorian era the presence or absence of the railway was crucial to the development of small towns.

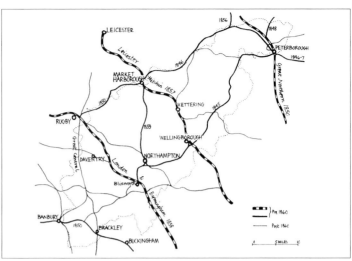

150 *The railways of Northamptonshire.*

In contrast to Daventry, Peterborough rose in importance, becoming the centre of a network of railways in the second phase of the development of the iron roads in the 1840s. In 1845 the Blisworth to Peterborough line (which passed through the south part of the town of Northampton) linked it to the London and Birmingham; just over a year later the Ely to Peterborough railway was constructed, followed in 1848 by the Peterborough to Boston and Lincoln line. Most important, the Great Northern railway from London to Doncaster reached the town in 1850, the section from Peterborough to Retford being built two years later. Generally, the earlier the railway came, the greater the development it engendered. In 1847 the *Northampton Herald* was reflecting ruefully, 'Northamptonshire is unfortunate in railway matters'.[24] This was true of Northampton on its minor branch line, and even more of Kettering and the central part of the county. In the 1840s depressed Kettering knew its future depended on the coming of the railway, and its hopes were raised and dashed more than once by the Midland Railway Company. In the event it had to wait until 1857 when the Leicester to Hitchin line was opened. The fortunes of the district then improved markedly; the footwear trade began to grow not only in Kettering, but also in the neighbouring towns and villages. The Leicester to Hitchin railway became the axis of this important part of the boot-and-shoe belt of Northamptonshire and indeed was a major reason for the rise of the trade there.

By the end of the 19th century a network of railways had been

151 *Celebrating the arrival of the Leicester to Hitchin line at Kettering in 1857.*

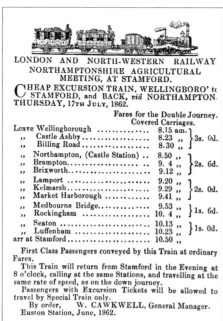

LONDON AND NORTH-WESTERN RAILWAY
NORTHAMPTONSHIRE AGRICULTURAL
MEETING, AT STAMFORD.
CHEAP EXCURSION TRAIN, WELLINGBORO' to
STAMFORD, and BACK, *viâ* NORTHAMPTON.
THURSDAY, 17TH JULY, 1862.

Fares for the Double Journey.
Covered Carriages.

Leave Wellingborough	8.15 am.	} 3s. 0d.
„ Castle Ashby	8.23 „	
„ Billing Road	8.30 „	
„ Northampton, (Castle Station) ..	8.50 „	} 2s. 6d.
„ Brampton.....................	9. 4 „	
„ Brixworth.....................	9.12 „	
„ Lamport	9.20 „	} 2s. 0d.
„ Kelmarsh.....................	9.29 „	
„ Market Harborough	9.41 „	
„ Medbourne Bridge.............	9.53 „	} 1s. 6d.
„ Rockingham	10. 4 „	
„ Seaton	10.13 „	} 1s. 0d.
„ Luffenham	10.23 „	
arr at Stamford...................	10.50 „	

First Class Passengers conveyed by this Train at ordinary Fares.
This Train will return from Stamford in the Evening at 8 o'clock, calling at the same Stations, and travelling at the same rate of speed, as on the down journey.
Passengers with Excursion Tickets will be allowed to travel by Special Train only.
By order,   W. CAWKWELL, General Manager.
Euston Station, June, 1862.

152 The benefits of the railway. Details of a 'cheap excursion train' to the Agricultural Show at Stamford in 1862.

constructed in Northamptonshire, the last line to be built being the Great Central through Brackley and Woodford Halse in 1899. However, in the story of industrial development the important railways were the early ones, and the fact that the county was 'unfortunate in railway matters' was one determinant of the extent and timing of the growth of its industries and the expansion of its towns. Another was how the local railways fitted into the national pattern. One reason why Leicester overtook Northampton in the second half of the 19th century as the greatest provincial shoe-making and distributing centre was its better position in the railway system. Northampton stood forlornly on its branch lines until 1882, and even then it was only on a secondary line and its communications with the North-East, Wales and the West remained much inferior to Leicester's.

Industrial Northamptonshire

By the reign of Queen Victoria Northamptonshire had become famous for its footwear industry. However, the making of boots and shoes for more than local needs was, for centuries, almost entirely confined to the town of Northampton. As we have seen, as late as 1777 there were far more weavers in Northamptonshire than shoemakers. It was in the forty or so years which followed that the making of footwear for the wholesale market expanded and spread to Wellingborough, Kettering, Earl's Barton, Finedon, Higham Ferrers, Raunds, Rushden, Wollaston and Daventry, and the nearby villages. This expansion was largely the result of the placing of contracts in Northamptonshire by the War Office and Admiralty, and by exporters to the colonies, in a period of almost continual war in Europe and the Empire.

In the following century the trade went through three stages of development: a long period of slow expansion in which output was increased by expanding the labour force, and by modifying (but not replacing) traditional methods; a transitional period from about 1859 in which machines were slowly introduced into more and more of the shoe-making processes, but in which most of the work still remained outside the factory; and the years from 1895 when it became predominantly a factory industry. It can be seen at once that the expansion of this trade had its own chronology, significantly different from that of other great industries of the time.

With the fall in demand after the end of the Napoleonic Wars the trade ceased to expand for a time, except at Northampton, and, to a lesser extent, at Wellingborough. The reason for Northampton's growth was that, from 1812, following labour troubles in London, the wholesalers began to put out work to the town. In the next few years Northampton was able to capture London's export trade in cheap footwear. In 1815 a consortium of Northampton manufacturers opened a warehouse in the capital, and the link was strengthened when the arm of the Grand Junction canal was opened that year. Thereafter Northampton emerged as the first great provincial centre of the wholesale footwear manufacture. In the 19th century shoe-making

153 *Northampton shoemakers, about 1866.*

dominated Northampton: in 1831 one man in three was engaged in the trade, and by 1871 the proportion had risen to two in five. Northampton dominated the trade in the county and never lost its dominance: 40 per cent of the shoemakers were concentrated there in 1831; 70 years later the proportion was still the same.

What attracted the London wholesalers to Northamptonshire was the cheapness of labour. In order to keep it cheap female and child workers were introduced on a large scale. In addition, output was increased by the introduction of the division of labour into a trade in which traditionally the making of shoes was carried out from start to finish by a single craftsman. In Northampton, children, often as young as six and seven, were taught stabbing and stitching, men doing the knife-work and tooling. Whole families laboured together in their own homes, or in the shops of garret-masters, who ruthlessly ground down wages. Whilst these developments increased output, they debased the position of the hand-sewn shoemaker, who found it near impossible to command good wages or combine to improve his position. The trade was in the hands of a large number of small masters, and the small-master tradition was very important in Victorian Northampton. They often started in the trade without much capital, and were frequently forced out by the keenness of the competition. They organised the work on the domestic system, and their warehouses or 'factories' were little more than 'putting-out stations'. Most were Dissenters in religion and Whig or Liberal in politics. By the 1830s they were numerous enough to mount a challenge to the Church-and-Tory power-structure in the borough.

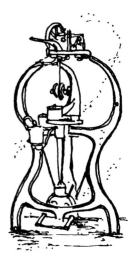

154 *Blake sole-sewer, c.1890, Northampton Museum.*

155   Northampton's first new shoe factory, Manfields', on Campbell Square, erected 1857.

Decade by decade the trade in the county grew. In 1851 there were 13,000 shoemakers, and by the end of that decade its first phase of development was reaching its end. The next began with the introduction of the first machine into the trade. In 1857 the pressures of competition led some Northampton manufacturers to attempt to replace hand-sewing with machine-sewing in the closing of the shoe uppers. This attempt was met with determined resistance, organised on a county-wide basis by the shoemakers, who feared the sewing machine would rob them of the wages of their children, and turn them (the men) into factory workers. This was not overcome for more than a year (1857-9). But in the end the closing machine came in, closing became women's work, and small specialist 'closers to the trade' opened workshops where women and children made nothing but uppers. From this time shoe uppers became the particular speciality of Wellingborough. In this period there were two other significant developments. In 1857 the important Leicester-Hitchin railway was opened, and in 1861 the technique of riveting the uppers to the soles of men's heavy boots, in place of stitching, was patented. Both of these had much to do with the expansion of the trade in Kettering and district. At last the town began to emerge from the prolonged depression which had started in the 1790s. Specialising in heavy rivetted working boots, the town grew so rapidly that by 1881 it had overtaken Wellingborough as the second largest footwear centre in the county. Rivetting and the railway brought an even more spectacular development in Leicester. From having virtually no footwear industry at all in 1850 it had, within a generation, overtaken Northampton as the main provincial centre of production.

156   A machine closer's premises in Northampton, 1869.

Events in the early 1870s gave a further stimulus to footwear in Northamptonshire. At the time of the Franco-Prussian War the French government placed immense orders for army boots and these were followed by others for the home market in the great boom of 1871-4. The result was a very considerable growth in the industry, which was to be sustained into the 1880s and 1890s. In these decades there was a gradual increase in the numbers of machines coming into use in the production of footwear, and in the end the trade became a

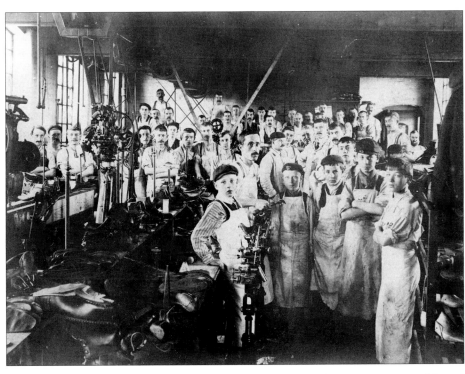

157 *Kettering footwear workers in the factory of Henry Hanger, Junior, St Andrew's Street, about 1885.*

factory-based industry. At first, however, increased output was achieved by an extension of traditional methods, not by machinery; the years 1870 to 1895 saw a vast increase in hand-work and small-scale production. A ready supply of workers was available because this was the time when the rural labourers, faced with the great agricultural depression, began to leave the land in droves. This ready availability of labour ensured that wages were kept low, and the intensely competitive nature of the industry forced them even lower, leading to the widespread use of 'boy labour', the 'team system' of production, and the employment of 'assistants' by the outworkers. On the eve of the factories shoe-making was more than ever a sweated industry. It was for this reason that the Rivetters and Finishers Union (the forerunner of the modern National Union of Footwear, Leather, and Allied Trades) was formed in 1874. For some years it remained very weak in Northamptonshire.

158 *Footwear Union membership certificate, 1880s.*

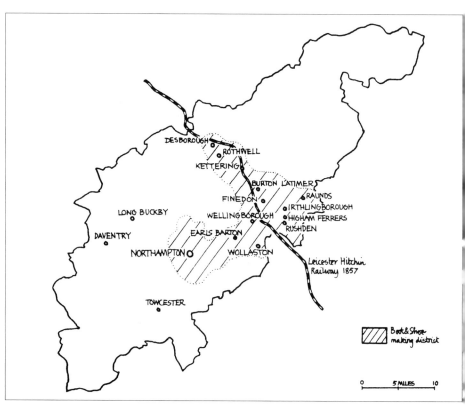

159 *The location of the main footwear centres in Northamptonshire.*

The union realised that so long as outwork and its abuses persisted the workers would never materially improve their wages and conditions. But its work was doubly difficult: not only was it weak vis-à-vis the employers, it was hampered by the widespread opposition of the workers to the idea of working in factories. The end of the second phase in the development of the industry was marked by the bitter 'Boot War' of 1895 between the union and the employers. The union lost the 'war', but from then on the industry was not destined to be beset by further serious labour troubles. One reason was that it rapidly became a factory industry after 1895, and the union found it easier to establish a lasting basis for collective bargaining than when outwork was the basis of the industry.

Footwear was the only industry of any size in Victorian Northamptonshire. Some engineering developed in Northampton, Kettering and Wellingborough, and the introduction of the sewing-machine in the 1850s led to a clothing industry establishing itself at Kettering and Desborough. Following the interest in local ironstone aroused by the Great Exhibition of 1851, mining of this material commenced, and at different times was carried on at 75 quarries in the county. And following the experiments of William Butlin in 1852-3 in smelting this local ore a number of small ironworks were opened. In 1898 there were some 27 furnaces at eight different places producing pig-iron, but by the time of the Great War output was in decline. And, compared with the 42,000 shoemakers and the 11,600 agricultural workers in 1901, the numbers engaged in engineering, clothing, quarrying and iron production in Northamptonshire were very small.

The footwear trade was of great historic importance to Northamptonshire. Had the trade not developed when it did, and in the way it did, the county would have remained predominantly agricultural and been forced to witness the large-scale migration of its people to the industrial areas, or abroad. As it was, foot-wear's growth was very largely generated from within. With the exception of individuals, such as M.P. Manfield, who emigrated from Bristol to Northampton in the 1840s, people were not drawn in large numbers from much beyond the county boundaries. Yet important though the trade was, its size and impact should not be over-exaggerated. By 1881 it had been overtaken by Leicester, and the arrival of the factories virtually coincided with the end of its growth as an employer of labour. In this respect it reached its peak just after the death of Queen Victoria. Output, of course, continued to expand for the next 60 years, and both World Wars gave a great stimulus to Northamptonshire's staple industry.

160 *Clothing manufacture: the Co-operative Wholesale Society's Corset Factory, Desborough. Underwear, though not corsets, is still made here.*

Nor, perhaps, should its scope as an agent of change be exaggerated. It was confined geographically to particular parts of the county, and, even within those, generated only a modest amount of town growth. Northampton grew most of all; in the century from 1801 it increased from 7,000 to 87,000, but Kettering only grew from 3,000 to 29,000, and Wellingborough from about the same figure of 18,000. By the standards of Industrial Britain in the 19th century none ranked as even a moderately large town. All this meant that the rural character of the county and its people persisted not only through the Victorian era but also well into the 20th century.

Politics and Elections

Between the Reform Act of 1832 and the present time local politics and elections in Northamptonshire follow the general shift in the context of national politics. They reflect the transition from a time when politics were dominated by local social and political élites to the present situation in the mass society, where politics has divided along the lines of class and increasingly reflect the supremacy of national over local issues.

Before the 1832 Reform Act the Northamptonshire constituencies returned nine members to parliament: two 'knights of the shire', two

161 *The arms of Sir Rainald Knightley.*

162 *Prominent Whig politician: John Charles, 3rd Earl Spencer (1782-1845)*

burgesses each for the boroughs of Northampton, Brackley and Peterborough, and one for Higham Ferrers. They were elected on a variety of franchises: from Northampton, where there was virtual democracy, the electors including all the inhabitant householders, paying 'scot and lot' and not in receipt of poor relief, down to the mere 33 voters in both Brackley and Higham Ferrers. The two county members were elected by the 40-shilling freeholders, of whom there were about 8,000 in 1832. The seven borough members in the early 19th century were the nominees of great Whig families—the Spencers and the Bouveries at Northampton, the Fitzwilliams at Peterborough and Higham, and the Dukes of Bridgewater at Brackley. In the 18th century the Tory squires regarded the boroughs as the sphere of the Whig aristocrats and the county seats as theirs, but, since the famous intervention of Lord Althorp in the election of 1806, to avoid contests the pattern had been to return one Whig (Althorp himself) and one Tory squire, W.R. Cartwright of Aynho. In the contested 'Reform Election' of 1831 a second Whig, Viscount Milton

163 *Prominent Tory politician: William Ralph Cartwright of Aynho, Member of Parliament from 1797 to 1841, except for 1831-2.*

(Earl Fitzwilliam's heir), was, to the bitter chagrin of the squires, elected to serve with Althorp. So in the House of Commons which passed the Reform Act there was no local Tory' representation at all. Yet, bitterly though the Tory squires opposed Reform, its effects proved anything but unkind to their political prospects. The Whig pocket boroughs of Higham and Brackley were disfranchised, and the number of county seats were doubled; this meant that if the Tories were able to reorganise and reassert their old primacy in the rural areas they might well be able to win four of the eight Northamptonshire seats in parliament. And this is what happened. In its local context Whig Reform turned out uncommonly conservative.

Between 1837 and 1880 the North and South Northants constituencies almost invariably returned Tories to the House of Commons, the only exception being a short-lived Spencer victory in the South in 1857. The continuation of the old squire-dominated arrangements under which successive Cartwrights and Knightleys in the South, and Burghleys, and the representatives of such local families as the Maunsells and Ward-Hunts in the North, were elected made it seem that the 18th century lasted until 1880 in Northamptonshire. The Liberal victory of the Hon. C.R. Spencer in that year in North Northants came as a reminder that democracy was just around the corner, though the long political Indian summer of the squires was simply a reflection of the fact that the forces of economic and social change had largely by-passed rural Northamptonshire. Moreover, democracy was not something that could not be adjusted to; whatever was abolished in 1884-5, it was not deference.

In the two borough constituencies the Whigs remained the dominant party after the Reform Act. In Northampton, after a brief period in the early 1830s when a Tory managed to win one of the seats, the pattern of a candidate acceptable to the borough Whigs and a Liberal acceptable to the Dissenters and shoe-manufacturers was settled on. There

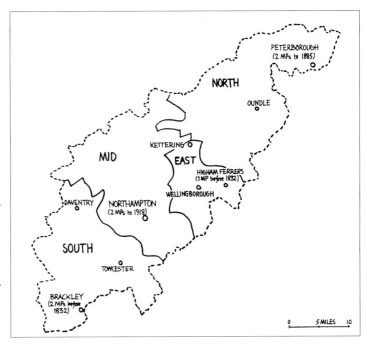

164 *Parliamentary constituencies in Northamptonshire in 1885.*

165 *Pickering Phipps, Northampton brewer and leading churchman and Conservative.*

was, however, always a Radical presence in the borough, which emerged as a significant force when some working-men got the vote in 1867. The result was the famous challenge to the Whig-Liberal party mounted by Charles Bradlaugh, newspaperman, republican, atheist, champion of civil liberties, advocate of birth-control and hero of the Radicals, who first stood for parliament in Northampton in 1868. His candidature at the 1874

166 *Statue to Charles Bradlaugh, Abington Square, Northampton, erected 1894. Bradlaugh was Radical MP for Northampton from 1880 until his death in 1891.*

election so divided the Liberal vote that Pickering Phipps, a local brewer, was elected, the first Tory since 1835. Clearly Bradlaugh had to be accommodated: eventually the party split was healed, a new United Liberal Party was formed, and in 1880 Labouchere and Bradlaugh, a highly successful partnership, were returned to Westminster. There followed the celebrated constitutional episode when Bradlaugh was excluded by the House of Commons when he tried to affirm instead of taking the oath. Four times the electors returned him at elections in a remarkable assertion of the right of constituencies to elect whom they wanted to parliament, and it was the House of Commons, and not Bradlaugh and Northampton, which gave way in the end. Bradlaugh took his seat in 1886, and represented the borough until his death in 1891.

Following the third instalment of Reform in 1884-5, which gave the vote to the rural male householder, the county was divided into four single-member constituencies, Peterborough was reduced to a single-member borough, while Northampton retained its two members. Down to the Great War, of the four rural seats North Northants and South Northants remained generally safely Conservative, whilst Mid Northants, much of which was Spencer territory, and East Northants were Liberal. Indeed, the latter, which included Kettering, Wellingborough and the smaller towns of the boot-and-shoe belt, was one of the safest, if not *the* safest, Liberal seats in Britain. Northampton, too, remained solidly Liberal in this period, and Peterborough generally went that way at elections, though it was Unionist between 1895 and 1906. However, in 1906 in the landslide Liberal victory of that election, the first of the local Lib-Lab candidates, in the person of George Nicholls, got in there.

The Liberal tradition remained strong in Northamptonshire until the Great War, but proved no more resistant than elsewhere to those circumstances which brought about the party's collapse—the split when Lloyd George became Prime Minister in 1916 and its perpetuation in the election of 1918, the determination of the Labour Party to go its own way, the decline of religious Dissent and of the family-business tradition. Its collapse locally came between the announcement by Kettering's Liberal M.P. in 1916 that in future he would not stand against the Labour Party, and Earl Spencer becoming a Conservative in 1924. From the

167 *Detail of the former Liberal Club, Kettering.*

time of the redistribution of seats in 1918, when Northampton became a one-member constituency (the others being Kettering, Wellingborough and the two rural seats of Daventry and Peterborough), politics polarised around class, and increasingly elections turned on the great issues of national politics. The rural seats have generally been Conservative: Daventry (the old South and Mid Northants constituencies) wholly so; Peterborough generally so, though falling to Labour in the great electoral swings of 1929 and 1945. Kettering and Wellingborough both went over to Labour in 1918, and have since been generally Labour-held when the party has done well nationally, as in 1918, 1927, 1929 and 1945. In Northampton the Liberals survived as a force a little longer: it was not until 1923 that Labour first captured the seat. Until very recently, however, it has generally been held by Labour, though it had a Conservative M.P. in 1924-9, 1931-45 and 1979-97.

168 *Margaret Bondfield, a women's trade union organiser and MP for Northampton 1923-4. The first woman to hold a Cabinet post.*

The changes in English society generally in the last three decades or so, and the local growth of population and new industry have been followed by changes in the results of recent elections in Northamptonshire. It seems that since the later 1960s a new phase of political history has been entered. If politics continue to follow class, and the county continues to remain part of the prosperous South-East, as seems likely, it is hard to escape the conclusion that Northamptonshire will continue to depart more and more from its old Liberal and Labour political traditions.

The Development of Local Government

In 1974 a system of local government which had lasted for 80 years was replaced by the one we have now. The 1894 system had in its turn replaced an older form of government which had been modified by the piecemeal process of 19th-century Reform, but which, in its origins, was much older.

On the eve of the first Reform Act the central government played a distant role in the local government of England: it is a truism that local government then was truly local. The county was overseen by Justices of the Peace sitting in Quarter Sessions when, before the business of the courts was transacted, they regulated certain matters of county government, principally those concerning the administration of justice, the county gaol and bridges over rivers. At that time government at county level

169 *Daventry Moot Hall.*

170 *Towcester Town Hall, 1865.*

171 *Newspaper notice about the Harleston Association for the Prosecution of Felons' bloodhounds, 1812.*

was minimal, and administration was largely in the hands of local bodies in the villages and towns. Village government was usually carried out by two bodies—the manorial court and the parish vestry. At the infrequent meetings of these bodies the parish and manorial officers—the overseers of the poor, the surveyors of highways, the parish constables, and so on—were appointed, and village government was in the hands of local ratepayers. Although the local Justice of the Peace was there to be appealed to in such matters as poor law disputes, it was not the custom to interfere directly in the workings of parish government. In towns the situation was more complicated. In Northampton, Daventry, Brackley and Higham Ferrers, all boroughs incorporated by royal charter, the functions of government were usually divided between the borough corporation, the parish vestry, or vestries, and the manorial court, if there still was one. Having their own Justices and courts to oversee law and order, the boroughs were largely independent of the country gentlemen. Towns without corporations, such as Wellingborough, Kettering and Peterborough were usually governed in much the same way as villages, by manorial court and parish vestry, and had to look to the county Justices of the Peace for petty-sessional justice.

By 1832 the limitations of old-style local government were well known; both in boroughs and unincorporated towns its agencies were inadequate to the task of providing the services reformers were coming to demand of local government. There were many reasons for this, but in part this was because they lacked the necessary legal powers; the corporation of the borough of Northampton could not become a paving or sewerage authority because its charters did not give it the power. By 1832 something had, in fact, been done about this sort of problem: Boards of Improvement Commissioners set up by local Acts of Parliament were at work in Northampton, Oundle, Peterborough and Daventry to carry out improvements the other town authorities were not empowered to undertake. Similarly other *ad hoc* bodies had come into existence, or were shortly to do so, to carry out functions, later generations were to see as part and parcel of local government— Turnpike Trusts, Felons' Associations, and private enterprise Gas and Water Companies.

Following the Reform Act of 1832 the Whigs introduced some changes in local government. The first was the Poor Law Amendment Act of 1834. As we have seen, this took the relief of the poor away from the individual parish. Twelve poor law unions were set up in North-amptonshire, and almost by accident became authorities on to which local government functions could be grafted. The following year the Municipal Corporations Act became law. Its principal objective was to replace closed Tory corporations with municipal councils elected by, and responsible to, the ratepayers. The corporations of Northampton and Daventry were abolished, but those of Brackley and Higham Ferrers (both in the pockets of Whig lords) survived into the 1880s. In Daventry the Tories still remained dominant after 1835. In Northampton, though the first borough council election resulted in equal numbers of Whigs and Tories being returned, the Whigs soon came to dominate the council, a reflection in politics of the rise of the Dissenters and manufacturers. The third development was the formation of the county police force in 1839. Before that time, Northamptonshire, like most of the rest of England, was virtually self-policing, though the inadequacies of the system whereby unpaid ratepayers acted as parish constable for a

172 *Northampton's new Guildhall, 1861-4. One of the first in the newly fashionable Gothic style, the work of Edward Godwin. It was extended in the same style in 1889-92 by the local architect, Matthew Holding.*

year had long been felt. In fact, since about 1790 local Associations for the Prosecution of Felons had grown up in a voluntary effort to improve the system of investigating and punishing crimes against property. At first there was strong opposition to a paid police force from the Justices of the Peace, who feared a 'rural gendarmerie' responsible to the Home Office and not to themselves and suspected that paid police might be followed by a paid magistracy.

Important though these reforms were, they did little to make the pattern of local government any simpler or more efficient. The reform of local institutions was not something Victorian governments at Westminster were very interested in. Yet people were coming to demand improved local services such as street-paving and draining, pure water, improved sanitation, the provision of cemeteries, and eventually even elementary schools for all children. As far as new local government bodies to provide these were concerned, what followed was more of the same. Under the provision of various statutes, especially the 1848 and

173 *Local government authorities, 1894 to 1974.*

1858 Public Health Acts, local boards began to proliferate. By the 1870s there were Burial Boards, Highways Board, School Boards, Rural Sanitary Boards in the country, and Local Government Boards in the towns. While these gradually came to improve local services, the 'board' system had shortcomings. These Acts were usually permissive: Wellingborough adopted a Board of Public Health, but the obstructive ratepayers of Kettering refused to have one. In the '70s, at long last, the central government began to use its influence more directly in local government. Under the powers granted by the Public Health Act of 1872 and the Local Government Act of 1875 (which for the first time set up a board at Whitehall to oversee what was happening at the local level), it forced recalcitrant towns such as Kettering to modernise their local government.

The next step was the reform of county and parish government. This went against the wishes of the landowners—Lord Salisbury once sarcastically said it was not parish councils that were needed, but parish circuses—and was resisted until after the franchise was extended to the rural labourer in 1884-5. Only then could the self-selective system of the magistracy, who spent the ratepayers' money without having to answer to them, be reformed. The long reign of the J.P.s in Quarter Sessions came to an end in 1888 when the County Councils Act was passed. In Northamptonshire in that year a council of 51 elected councillors and 17 nominated aldermen started its work under the chairmanship of Earl Spencer. Six years later, under the Parish Councils Act, the vestries were replaced by elected parish councils and the boards in small towns by Urban District Councils. The Rural Sanitary Boards, set up in the 1870s in the poor law unions, were taken over by Rural District Councils. Following the County Councils Act the Soke of Peterborough severed its ancient connection with Northamptonshire and went its own way. In modern times it has not preserved this independence; in 1965 it was forcibly wedded to the county of Huntingdon, and in 1974 became part of Cambridgeshire, when that county absorbed Huntingdonshire.

Between 1894 and 1974 local government in the county was essentially divided between the boroughs and the county council. By the second third of the 20th century it became clear, with the spread of motor car ownership, suburbanisation, and the movement of townspeople into the villages, that this division into town and country, rural and urban, was becoming progressively less in accord with social reality. People were living in the country and paying the lower county rates, but working in the towns and using facilities provided by the borough councils. In addition it was argued that there were too many small units in local government, and that fewer and bigger units would result in more and better services, and bring the benefits of economies of scale. For 40 years the reform of local government was debated. Royal Commissions sat, reported, and saw their Reports ignored. Services, meanwhile, refused to wait on authorities; from the end of the Second World War giant regional electricity, gas, water and hospital authorities were created outside the framework of local government. In 1966 this trend came closer when the Northampton borough and county police forces were amalgamated on the orders of the Home Secretary. Finally, following the Maud Report of 1969, the 1972 Local Government Act was passed, and two years later the modern Northamptonshire County Council came into being. Under it the four boroughs and 18 district councils of the old County Council were replaced by a more powerful County Council, with the old boroughs reduced to the status of being merely four of the seven 'second tier' authorities.

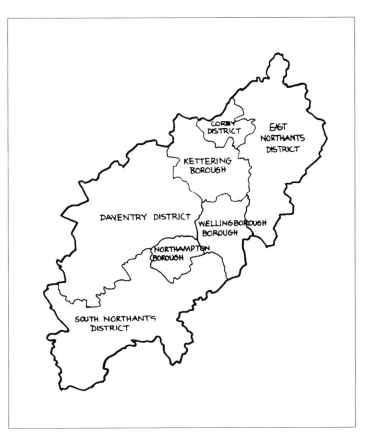

174 *Local government authorities since 1974.*

6

Twentieth-Century Developments

The 20th-century history of Northamptonshire fell into three phases: the years from the end of Queen Victoria's reign in 1901 to the beginning of the Second World War, a period when the county can be said to have been marking time; the years from about 1940 to the opening of the Ml motorway in 1959, when the economy of modern Northamptonshire began to diversify, and new industries and occupations came along which modified the traditional dependence on footwear; and the modern era of planned growth and office-based industries which emerged since about 1960. These developments are reflected in the growth of Northamptonshire's population: between 1901 and 1939 it grew by only eight per cent; between 1939 and 1961 it grew by 20 per cent; and between 1961 and the present it increased by 55 per cent.

The reasons for the relative lack of growth in the first 40 years of the century lay generally with the continuing decline in agriculture, the reduced size of the English family, the inter-war Depression, and the fact that in the early years of the century the footwear industry reached its peak as an employer of labour. Against this it must be said that Northamptonshire did not suffer from unemployment of the severity of that in the older centres of heavy industry. Although the period of expansion only really began after (or perhaps during) the Second World War, some developments which paved the way for it had their origins in the inter-war years. One such was at Corby. The start of its transformation was in 1880 when Samuel Lloyd (1827-1918) took a lease on the deposits of ironstone on the estates of the Countess of Cardigan in the district. At first the project was to mine the raw material for smelting elsewhere, but in 1907 a new Lloyd company was formed to set up furnaces at Corby, and three years later the first cast of pig-iron was made there. However, production remained small-scale until the '30s, when Stewart and Lloyds, a Scottish firm, acquired the assets of several local iron and ironstone companies, and as an act of deliberate economic planning decided to locate their major steel-tube plant on the ironstone beds of Northamptonshire, a decision which cost £3¾ million to implement. The Corby plant was built to produce 'Basic Bessemer quality' steel, and in 1934 No. 1 blast furnace was lit. Corby was rapidly transformed from a village into a steel town, with a garden suburb which housed the workers and their families, many of whom

175 *Northampton engineering British Timken tapered roller-bearings.*

came with the firm from Scotland. By 1939 Corby's population had grown from a mere 1,500 to 10,000.

176 *Aerial photograph of Corby Steel Works in 1974. All this has now gone.*

From the end of the Second World War Northamptonshire's fortunes have increasingly been caught up in those of the prosperous South-east of England. The first indication of this was when, in 1950, Corby was designated one of the first post-war New Towns. Its Development Corporation's first target was to expand it to a town of 40,000, and by 1963 had done so. Already the second largest town in the county, it was then given a new target figure, and the designation area was enlarged; by 1977 it had reached its new target of 55,000. Yet, although some new industries came to Corby, it remained overwhelmingly a one-industry town—some 12,000 people depended on British Steel for their livelihood there.

For a time Corby New Town seemed an exception—a planted town, dreamed up in London, but only a portent of the future. What really brought Northamptonshire closer to the prosperous South-East was the building of the Ml motorway, completed in 1959. Out of the blue, the old historical connection between Northampton's fortunes and the national road system revealed itself again. The county found itself in the middle of the new motorway network. This was particularly true of Northampton.

177 *Expanding North-ampton: the Weston Favell Centre, 1979.*

Since the war the town had seen its labour force in the footwear industry fall by about a half, though its total output of shoes kept up. The trade in Northampton was by now concentrating on good quality footwear, and exporting half its output. However, since the late 1930s Northampton's industrial pattern had been changing. By 1959 light engineering had become the biggest employer, with a workforce of 13,000, about as many as there had been in footwear at the end of the war. But since then light engineering in its turn has been overtaken by service industries—distribution, warehousing and professional services (particularly the growth of all branches of public administration)—as the major employer. The viability of the local economy, Northampton's low rate of unemployment (consistently half the national average rate) and its potential as a distribution centre, were reasons why the government planners began to take interest in it. In the *South East Study* of 1965 Northampton was designated one of the New Towns to take people and industries from London, a scheme financed directly from the Treasury. In 1968 a Development Corporation was appointed to expand Northampton's population from about 120,000 to 230,000 by 1981. It was by then expected to have an economy in which two in every three jobs would be in service industries. The first stages in the creation of the new Northampton (primarily developments on the east and north-east of the town, paralleled by much 'urban renewal' in the older parts of the town), were carried out with impressive precision.

In close proximity to the motorway system, virtually all the towns in the Greater Northampton area were seen by the planners as having either natural, or stimulated, growth potential. In the latter category, Wellingborough, although not given a Development Corporation, was, like Corby and Northampton, encouraged to expand as an overspill town for Greater London. The emphasis was to have been on developing the shoe trade which, alas! was beginning to decline, but a certain amount of new industry was attracted. However, its planned growth from 32,000 to 80,000 people by 1981 was not achieved. The borough of Daventry, arguably the place most in need of an economic stimulus in Northamptonshire, received one from a provincial (as opposed to a London) source. An expansion scheme linked with Birmingham's desire to decentralise industry and people was devised, and in 1963 a Development Corporation started work there. A thousand acres of land around the town were bought, and houses, schools and factories erected, and the population rapidly increased from 6,000 to 14,500. Given its experience of a century's stagnation, the development of Daventry was, in many ways, an impressive achievement, but the scheme did not go as planned, many Birmingham firms were unwilling to move, and the target population of 36,000 by 1981 has never been achieved. Somewhat further afield, major development schemes at Peterborough and Milton Keynes were carried through.

The era of New Towns came to an end in 1979 at the hands of a Government which saw central planning as 'socialistic'. There was an immediate policy of cutting public expenditure from which few areas emerged unscathed. Northampton and Corby Development Corporations were wound up, whilst at Daventry the arrangements with Birmingham had ended in 1976 when that City pulled out of the project, though the plans there were completed. The achievements of this era were major ones. The population of the county rose by 71,000 in the '60s and 58,000 in the '70s, vast housing developments were built to accommodate the newcomers, new sources of employment attracted and great improvements effected in the road system. In retrospect, it is clear that, with the decline of footware manufacturing and other old sources of employment, modern Northamptonshire would have been in a sorry state if these developments had not gone ahead. Not all the targets of the planners were achieved, largely because of recessions and balance-of-payments crises in the nation's affairs. Planning was always predicated on estimates of the performance of the economy

178 New roads: the Nene Valley Way at Wootton under construction in 1974.

as a whole, and it is the achievement of the British economy never to perform to expectations.

At the start of the Thatcherite era there were serious setbacks locally, the greatest of which was the decision of the British Steel Corporation to end its operations in Corby. The loss of 6,000 jobs, which meant casting a quarter of the town's labour force into unemployment, was a devastating blow to the local economy. Yet Corby rapidly transformed itself. A £53 million plan to attract new businesses was put into operation by the District Council and

179 New roads: the M1/A1 Link, now A14, near Naseby in 1999.

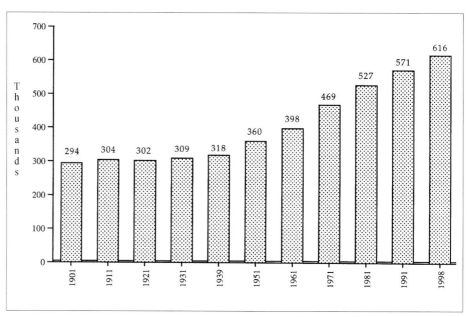

180 *The population of Northamptonshire, 1901 to 1998.*

the Development Corporation. Corby bounced back. The same could not be said for Northamptonshire's footware industry, which continued to decline in the face of the flood of cheap foreign imports. Yet, even here, the firm of Griggs, manufacturers of the famous 'Dr Martin' boots, flourished where others declined. Apart from them, the only footware firms which have kept going are those making shoes for the more expensive end of the market.

Conservative governments directed economic policy into new directions. Yet if development now had to be a partnership between local authorities and the private sector, with the balance being with the latter, planned growth continued, if no longer on the previous scale. An example of this co-operation was the way that Kettering, largely by-passed by new developments in the previous decades, responded to the local crisis caused by government cuts, the closure of Corby Works and the decline of footware. In 1982 nearly one in four males was jobless. An industrial strategy identified sites in private ownership for factory and high technology developments. Small firms, together with major companies such as Weetabix expanding in the district, pointed the way forward. To firms and people considering re-locating there, Kettering stressed its good communications and reasonable house prices, and it did attract people from the South-East. Soon there were 500 daily commuters by rail to London. A further boost came with the go-ahead of the M1/A1 road scheme, a project of national importance, linking as it does the West Midlands and the East Coast ports.

Despite the continuation of the cycle of boom and recession, in the two decades since 1979 the population of the county continued to grow. In the '80s it did so by 44,000, in the '90s by 45,000. In percentage terms this was an increase of 17 per cent, against the 32 per cent of the previous two decades. The old economy has been replaced by the new. The number of shoeworkers has shrunk to an estimated 6,700, and there is little if any heavy industry left. People now work in service industries, food processing and retailing, and local government and the Health Service are large employers. With new housing developments being located on the edges of towns, in expanded small towns such as Rothwell and villages like Long Buckby, the old town centres are increasingly being left to the poor. Their decline is accelerated by the popularity of out-of-town shopping, which invariably follows the

181 *Where shoe factories once stood: some of Northampton's unoccupied new offices.*

building of new roads and by-passes. The planners themselves can be caught out by this. Today, Northampton has an excess of office space. The assumption was that office-based employers would come in larger numbers than they did. Yet when they did come, it was often to locate on out-of-town developments. The planners themselves exemplified the trend. Local government offices have moved to the suburban edges. The life span of new urban buildings has an American brevity. In Northampton, Northampton House, the tallest high-rise block of the '70s built to house local government employees, lay empty since 1991; at the time of writing it is being converted into housing. The architecturally abysmal Barclaycards building, which rose up above the town in the early '70s has recently been demolished. Not far away, neo-Georgian offices near St Sepulchre's church have remained untenanted for nearly a decade.

A feature of modern society is that in many of its essentials—employment, housing, popular culture—it is becoming homogenised. One place is becoming much like another, especially in the South East. Yet not everything is engulfed by the new. Many years ago the late J.L. Carr listed his six most famous Northamptonshire things: 'Boots, the Battle of Naseby, cricketer V.W.C. Jupp, Earls Barton's church tower, Rushden brass band ... and the Saints' forwards in the loose'. Well, footwear is almost gone and no one who is not a cricket historian remembers Jupp. But the battle of Naseby will not be forgotten, Earls Barton's Saxon tower has not fallen down and there is still a brass band tradition. And, as I write (in the year 2000), it is only a few days since the Saints' forwards brought Rugby Union's European Cup back in triumph to Northampton.

References

1.   (page 18). Thomas Fuller, *Anglorum Speculum or The Worthies of England*, 1684, pp.533-4.
2.   (page 25). Tony Brown and Glenn Foard, 'The Saxon landscape: a regional perspective' in *The Archaeology of Landscape*, edited by P. Everson and T. Williamson, 1998, p.73. This essay is required reading on Anglo-Saxon Northamptonshire.
3.   (page 30). *Ibid.*, p.81.
4.   (page 41). K.J. Allison, M.W. Beresford, and J.G. Hurst, *The Deserted Medieval Villages of Northamptonshire*, 1966, p.41.
5.   (page 52). *V.C.H.*, II, Eccles. Hist.
6.   (page 53). 'Pretty Bank', *V.C.H.*, II.
7.   (page 54). Simon Gunton, *The History of the Church of Peterburgh*, 1686, pp.57-8.
8.   (page 56). Peter Gay, 'The Midland Revolt of 1607', *Transactions of the Royal Historical Society*, New Series, XVIII, 1904, p.217, fn. 1.
9.   (page 59). John Norden, *Speculae Britannia*, 1610 (1720), p.32.
10.   (page 60). *Ibid.*, p.29.
11.   (page 66). *V.C.H.*, II, 1906, p.43.
12.   (page 68). *V.C.H.*, II, p.52.
13.   (page 68). *Calendar of State Papers Domestic, Charles I, 1636-7*, pp.150-1.
14.   (page 69). *Calendar of State Papers Domestic, Charles I, 1640*, p.7.
15.   (page 77). E.G. Forrester, *Northamptonshire County Elections and Electioneering 1695 to 1832*, 1941, p.56.
16.   (page 81). *Manchester Guardian*, 12 April 1856.
17.   (page 82). Thomas Fuller, *Worthies, op.cit.*, p.534.
18.   (page 83). D. Defoe, A *Tour Through England and Wales*, Everyman edition, 1928, I, p.86.
19.   (page 83). *Ray's Itineraries*, 9 August 1658, quoted in *Northamptonshire Notes & Queries*, III, p.241; Defoe, *Tour*, I, p.86; 5; 'finest expression', Sir Gyles Isham in an article in *Northamptonshire Independent*, October 1975.
20.   (page 87). 'An Account of the Conventicles held in the 7 Western deaneries of the Diocese of Peterborough', NRO, Fermor Hesketh (Baker), MS 708.
21.   (page 92). V.A.Hatley (ed.), *Northamptonshire Militia Lists 1777*, 1973, xviii, table 5.
22.   (page 97). Rev. John Mastin, *The History & Antiquities of Naseby*, 1792, p.15.
23.   (page 101). *Ibid.*, p.51.
24.   (page 113). *Northampton Herald*, 24 March 1847.

Select Bibliography

The books and articles listed below have been useful in the compilation of this volume. The titles of books are shown in *italics*, and the titles of articles are placed between inverted commas.

ABBREVIATIONS

J.N.N.H.S.F.C. *Journal of the Northamptonshire Natural History Society and Field Club.*
N.P.&P. *Northamptonshire Past and Present.*
N.R.S. *Northamptonshire Record Society.*
R.C.H.M. *Royal Commission on Historical Monuments.*
V.C.H. *Victoria History of the County of Northampton.*

Adkins, W.R.D. and Serjeantson, the Rev. R.M. (eds.)., *V.C.H.*, I, 1902.
Adkins, W.R.D. and Serjeantson, the Rev. R.M. (eds.)., *V.C.H.*, II, 1906.
Allison, K.J., Beresford, M.W., and Hurst, J.G., *The Deserted Medieval Villages of Northamptonshire*, 1966.
Anscomb, J.W. 'Parliamentary Enclosure in Northamptonshire. Processes and Procedures', *N.P.&P.*, VII, 6, 1988-9, pp.409-24.
Anstruther, C., *Vaux of Harrowden*, 1953.
Arnstein, W.L., *The Bradlaugh Case*, 1965.
Artis, E.I., *The Durobrivae of Antoninus*, 1828.
Bailey's British Directory, 1784.
Baker, G.T., *The History and Antiquities of the County of Northampton*, I, 1823-30, II, 1836-41.
Barron, O., *Northamptonshire Families*, *V.C.H.*, 1906.
Barty-King, H., *Expanding Northampton*, 1985.
Bates, D.L. 'Cotton-Spinning in Northampton: Edward Cave's Mill, 1742-1761', *N.P.&P.*, IX, 3, 1996-7, pp.237-52.
Bates, D.L., 'Cotton-Spinning in Northampton: the Gibson & Forbes Mill, 1785-1806', *N.P.&P.*, 51, 1998, pp.57-75.
Bazeley, Margaret L., 'The Extent of the English Forest in the Thirteenth Century', *Trans. Royal Hist. Soc.*, IV, 1921.
Bearn W., 'Farming in Northamptonshire', *Jnl. Royal Ag. Soc.*, 1852.
Beaver, S.H., *Northamptonshire Land Use*, 1943 (part 58 of *The Land of Britain*, ed., L.D. Stamp).
Beaver, S.H., 'The Development of the Northamptonshire Iron Industry', in *London Essays in Geography*, 1951, ed. L.D. Stamp and A. Woolridge.
Beresford, M., *History on the Ground*, 1957 (repr. 1971).
Bowley, A.L. and Burnett-Hurst, A.R., *Livelihood and Poverty*, 1915.
Bridges, J., *The History and Antiquities of Northamptonshire* (ed. P. Whalley), 1791, 2 vols.
Brown, A.E., *Early Daventry*, 1991.
Brown. T. and Glenn Foard, 'The Saxon Landscape: a regional perspective' in *The Archaeology of Landscape*, ed. P. Everson and T. Williamson, 1998, pp.67-94.
Brundage, A.L., *The Making of the New Poor Law*, 1978.
Channing, F.A., *Memories of Midland Politics, 1885-1910*, 1918.
Collinson, P., *The Elizabethan Puritan Movement*, 1967.
Colvin, H.M. and Wodehouse, L.M., 'Henry Bell of King's Lynn and his work at Northampton', *Architectural History*, IV, 1961.
Cossons, A., 'The Turnpike Roads of Northamptonshire', *N.P.&P.*, 1, 3, 1950.

Cox, the Rev. J.C., 'Religious houses', in *V.C.H.*, II, 1906.

Cox, the Rev. J.C. and Serjeantson, the Rev. R.M., *History of the Church of the Holy Sepulchre, Northampton*, 1897.

Darby, H.C. and Terrett, I.B., *The Domesday Geography of Midland England*, 1971.

Dickens, A.G., 'Early Protestantism and the Church in Northamptonshire', *N.P.&P.*, VII, I, 1983-4, pp.27-39.

Donaldson, J., *General View of the Agriculture of the County of Northampton*, 1794.

Dornier, Ann (ed.), *Mercian Studies*, 1977.

Dyer, A., 'Northampton in 1524', *N.P.&P.*, VI, 2, 1979, pp.73-80.

Edgar, W., *Borough Hill, Daventry, and its History*, 1923.

Everitt, A., 'Social Mobility in Early Modern England', *Past and Present*, No.33, 1966.

Everitt, A., *The Local Community and the Great Rebellion*, 1969.

Everitt, A., *Change in the Provinces: the Seventeenth Century*, 1970.

Everitt, A., *Ways and Means in Local History*, 1971.

Finch, Mary, *Five Northamptonshire Families*, *N.R.S.*, Vol. 19, 1956.

Foard, G., 'The Administrative Organisation of Northamptonshire in the Saxon Period', *Anglo-Saxon Studies in Archaeology and History*, 4, 1985, pp.185-222.

Foard, G., 'The Saxon Bounds of Oundle', *N.P.&P.*, VIII, 3, 1991-2, pp.179-89.

Foard, G., 'Ecton: its lost village and landscape park', *N.P.&P.*, VIII, 5, 1993-4, pp.335-53.

Foard, G., 'The Civil War Defences of Northampton', *N.P.&P.*, IX, I, 1994-5, pp.4-45.

Foard, G., *Naseby; the Decisive Campaign*, 1995.

Foard, G., 'The Early Topography of Northampton and its Suburbs', *Northamptonshire Archaeology*, 26, 1995, pp. 109-22.

Forrester, E.G., *Northamptonshire County Elections and Electioneering 1695-1832*, 1941.

Fuller, T., *Worthies of England* (1661), 1840 ed.

Garmonsway, G.N. (ed.), *The Anglo-Saxon Chronicle* (Everyman ed.), 1967.

Gay, E.F., 'The Midland Revolt and the Inquisitions of Depopulation 1607', *Trans. Royal Hist. Soc.*, 1904.

Goddard., N., ' "A Sensation Without Parallel?": Reflections on the Third Earl Spencer's Northampton speech, November 1843', *N.P.&P.*, IX, 3, 1996-7, pp.265-72.

Goodfellow, P., 'Medieval Bridges in Northamptonshire', *N.P.&P.*, VII, 3, 1985-6, pp.143-58.

Goodfellow, P., 'Medieval Markets in Northamptonshire', *N.P.&P.*, VII, 5, 1987-8, pp.305-24.

Gordon, P., *Politics and Society: the Journals of Lady Knightley of Fawsley 1885 to 1913*, 1999.

Gover, J.E.B., Mawer, A. and Stenton, F.M., *The Place Names of Northants.*, 1933.

Greenall, R.L., 'Baptist as Radical: The Life and Opinions of the Rev. John Jenkinson of Kettering (1799-1876)', *N.P.&P.*, VIII, 3, 19912, pp.210-26.

Greenall, R.L., *Daventry Past*, 1999.

Greenall, R.L., 'The history of Boot and Shoemaking at Long Buckby', *N.P.&P.*, V, 5, 1977.

Greenall, R.L. (ed.), *The Kettering Connection-Northamptonshire Baptists and Overseas Missions*, 1993.

Greenall, R.L., 'The Rise of Industrial Kettering', *NP.&P.*, V, 3, 1975.

Greenall, R.L., 'Three nineteenth century agriculturalists', *N.P.&P.*, VII, 6, 1988-9, pp.443-5.

Greenall, R.L., 'Parson as man of affairs: the Rev. Francis Litchfield of Farthinghoe (1792-1876)', *N.P.&P.*, VIII, 2, 1990-1, pp.121-35.

Greenall, R.L. (ed.), *Philip Doddridge, Nonconformity and Northampton*, 1981.

Habakkuk, H.J., 'English Landownership 1680-1740', *Econ. Hist. Rev.*, 1940.

Hadley, W.W., 'Bradlaugh and Labouchere, an Episode in Constitutional History', *N.P.&P.*, II, 6, 1959.

Hall, D.N., 'Enclosure in Northamptonshire', *N.P.&P.*, IX, 4, 1997-8, pp.351-68.

Hall, D.N., *The Open Fields of Northamptonshire*, 1995.

Harris, P.J. and Hartop, P.W., *Northamptonshire. Its Land and People*, 1950.

Hart, C., 'Oundle: its province and eight hundreds', *N.P.&P.*, VIII, I, 1989-90, pp.3-23.

Hart, C., 'The Kingdom of Mercia', in *Mercian Studies* (ed. A. Dornier), 1977.

Hart, C., *The Hidation of Northamptonshire*, 1970.

Hart, C., 'The Peterborough Region in the Tenth Century: a Topographical Survey', *N.P. &P.*, VI, 1981-2, pp.243-5.

Hatley, V.A., 'Aspects of Northampton's History 1815-51', *N.P.&P.*, III, 6, 1965.

Hatley, V.A., 'Blaze at Buckby', *N.P. & P.*, IV, 2, 1967.

Hatley, V.A., 'Locks, lords and coal: a study in eighteenth century Northampton', *N.P.&P.*, VI,

4, 1980-1, pp.207-18.

Hatley, V.A., 'Monsters in Campbell Square', *N.P.&P.*, IV, 1, 1966.

Hatley, V.A., 'Northampton Re-vindicated: more light on why the Main Line missed the town', *N.P.&P.*, II, 6, 1959.

Hatley, V.A., *Northamptonshire Militia Lists, 1777*, *N.R.S.*, Vol. 25, 1973.

Hatley, V.A., *Snobopolis: Northampton in 1869*, 1966.

Hatley, V.A., *The St Giles' Shoe School*, 1966.

Hatley, V.A. and Rajczonek, A., *Shoemakers in Northamptonshire 1762-1911*, 1971.

Hoskins, W.G., *Midland England*, 1949.

Howarth, Janet, 'The Liberal Revival in Northamptonshire 1880-1895', *Hist. Jnl.*, XII, 1969.

Ireson, A. J., *Northamptonshire*, 1954.

Isham, Gyles, 'Sir Thomas Tresham and his Buildings', *Report and Papers of the Northants. Antiq. Soc.*, 1964-5.

Jacob, E.F., 'Henry Chichele', *N.P.&P.*, I, 1, 1948.

[James. T.], 'The History and Antiquities of the County of Northampton', *The Quarterly Review*, 101, 1857.

King, E., 'The Town of Peterborough in the Early Middle Ages', *N.P.&P.*, VI, 4, 1980-1, pp.187-95.

Lee, F., 'A New Theory of the Origins and Early Growth of Northampton', *Archaeological Jnl.*, 110, 1954.

Lee, H., 'MS. History of Northampton', reprinted in *J.N.N.H.S.F.C.*, 26, 1932.

The Liber Custumarum: the book of the Usages and Customs of the town of Northampton to 1448, 1895.

Markham, C.A., *The Stone Crosses of the County of Northampton*, 1901.

Markham, C.A. and Cox, the Rev. J.C., *The Records of the Borough of Northampton*, I and II, 1898.

Marks, R., *Medieval Stained Glass in Northamptonshire*, 1999.

Marlow, N., 'The Coming of the Railways to Northants.', *N.P.&P.*, III, 5, 1964.

Mellows, W.T. (ed.), *The Foundation of Peterborough Cathedral, 1541*, *N.R.S.*, Vol. 13, 1941.

Mellows, W.T. (ed.), *The Last Days of Peterborough Monastery*, *N.R.S.*, Vol. 12, 1947.

Mellows, W.T. (ed.), *The Chronicle of Hugh Candidus, a Monk of Peterborough*, 1949.

Morton, J., *Natural History of Northamptonshire*, 1712.

Mountfield, P.R., 'The Footwear Industry of the East Midlands', *East Midlands Geographer*, 3-4, 1962-67.

Neeson, J.M., *Commoners: Common Right, Enclosure and Social Change in England, 1700-1820*, 1993.

Norden, J., *Speculae Brittaniae Pars Altera: or, a Delineation of Northamptonshire* (1610), 1720.

Nuttall, G.F., *Calendar of the Correspondence of Philip Doddridge D.D. (1702-1751)*, 1979.

Osborne, Margaret, 'The Second Spring: Roman Catholicism in Victorian Northamptonshire', *N.P.&P.*, IX, I, 1994-5, pp.71-79.

Page, G., 'The Great Civil War: How it Began and Ended in Northamptonshire', *J.N.N.H.S.F.C.*, 28-9, 1937-8.

Parsons, D., 'Past History and Present Research at All Saints' Church, Brixworth', *N.P.&P.*, VI, 2, 1979, pp.61-71.

Pettit, P.A.J., *The Royal Forests of Northamptonshire 1558-1714*, *N.R.S.*, Vol. 23, 1968.

Pettit, P.A.J., 'Charles I and the Revival of Forest Law in Northamptonshire', *N.P.&P.*, III, 2, 1961.

Pevsner, N., *The Buildings of England: Northamptonshire* (revised ed.), 1974.

Peyton, S.A., *Kettering Vestry Minutes, 1799-1853*, *N.R.S.*, Vol. 6, 1933.

Pitt, W., *General View of the Agriculture of the County of Northampton*, 1809.

Return of the Owners of Land in England and Wales, 1873, Vol. II, 1875.

Rider Haggard, H., *Rural England*, Vol. II, 1906.

R.C.H.M., *An Inventory of the Historical Monuments in the County of Northampton*, I, Archaeological Sites in the North East of Northamptonshire, 1975.

R.C.H.M., *An Inventory of the Historical Monuments in the County of Northampton*, II, Archaeological Sites in Central Northamptonshire, 1979.

R.C.H.M., *An Inventory of the Historical Monuments in the County of Northampton*, III, Archaeological Sites in the North-West of Northamptonshire, 1981.

R.C.H.M., *An Inventory of the Historical Monuments in the County of Northampton*, IV,

Archaeological Sites in South-West Northamptonshire, 1982.

R.C.H.M., *An Inventory of the Historical Monuments in the County of Northampton*, V, An Inventory of Archaeological Sites and Churches in Northampton, 1985.

R.C.H.M., *An Inventory of the Historical Monuments in the County of Northampton*, VI, Architectural Sites in North Northamptonshire, 1984.

R.C.H.M., *Nonconformist Chapels and Meeting Houses Northamptonshire & Oxfordshire*, 1986.

R.C.H.M., *Peterborough New Town: A Survey of the Antiquities in the Areas of Development*, 1969.

R.C.H.M., *The Country Houses of Northamptonshire*, by John Heward and Robert Taylor, 1996.

Round, J. H., 'Introduction to the Northamptonshire Domesday', *V.C.H.*, I, 1902.

Royle, E., 'Charles Bradlaugh, Freethought and Northampton', *N.P.&P.*, VI, 3, 1980, pp.141-50.

Salzman, L.F. (ed.), *V.C.H.*, IV, 1937.

Scopes, Sir F., *The Development of Corby Works*, 1968.

Serjeantson, Rev. R.M., *History of the Church of All Saints, Northampton*, 1901.

Serjeantson, Rev. R.M., *History of the Church of St Peter, Northampton*, 1904.

Serjeantson, Rev. R.M., *History of the Church of St Giles, Northampton*, 1911.

Serjeantson, Rev. R.M. and Adkins, W.R.D., 'Ecclesiastical History', *V.C.H.*, II, 1906.

Serjeantson, the Rev. R.M. and Longden, the Rev. H.I., 'The Parish Churches and Religious Houses of Northamptonshire: Their Dedications, Altars, Images and Lights', *Archaeological Journal*, 70, 1913.

Sheils, W.J., *The Puritans in the Diocese of Peterborough 1558-1610*, N.R.S., Vol. 30, 1979.

Smith, Juliet, *Northamptonshire: A Shell Guide*, 1968.

Steane, J.M., *The Northamptonshire Landscape*, 1974.

Tate, W.E., 'Inclosure Movements in Northamptonshire', *N.P.& P.*, I, 2, 1949.

Thornton, J.H., 'The Northampton Cotton Industry—an Eighteenth Century Episode', *J.N.N.H.S.F.C.*, 33, 1959.

Tribe, D., *President Charles Bradlaugh, M.P.*, 1971.

Turner, G.J. (ed.), *Select Pleas of the Forest*, Selden Soc., XIII, 1901.

Universal British Directory of Trades and Commerce, 1791.

Williams, John H., Shaw, M. and Denharn, V., *Middle Saxon Palaces at Northampton*, 1985.

Williams, John H., 'Northampton's Medieval Guildhalls', *N.P.&P.*, VII, I, 1983-4, pp.5-9.

Williams, John H., *Saxon & Medieval Northampton*, Northampton Development Corporation, 1982.

Williams, J., 'The Early Development of the Town of Northampton', in *Mercian Studies* (ed. A. Dornier), 1977.

Wise, C., *The Montagus of Boughton and their Northamptonshire Homes*, 1888.

C.N. Wright's Commercial and General Directory and Blue Book of Northants., 1884.

Wake, J., *Northampton Vindicated: or Why the Main Line missed the Town*, 1935.

Wake, J., *The Brudenells of Deene*, 1953.

Whellan, W. & Co., *History, Gazetteer & Directory of Northants.*, 1849 & 1874.

Wykes, D.L., 'The church and early dissent: the 1669 return of Nonconformist Conventicles for the Archdeaconry of Northampton', *N.P.&P.*, VIII, 3, 1991-2, pp.197-209.

Index

Note: figures in **bold** refer to illustration numbers.